Late Night Calls

Prose Poems and Short Fiction

MARK VINZ

19 NEW RIVERS PRESS 92

Library of Congress Catalog Card Number 91-61263
ISBN 0-89823-138-8
Edited by C. W. Truesdale
Editorial Assistance by Paul J. Hintz
Cover photograph by Wayne Gudmundson
Book Design by Gaylord Schanilec
Typesetting by Peregrine Publications

The publication of *Late Night Calls* has been made possible by
generous grants from the Arts Development Fund of the United
Arts Council, the First Bank System Foundation, Liberty State
Bank, the Tennant Company Foundation, and the National En-
dowment for the Arts (with funds appropriated by the Con-
gress of the United States). New Rivers Press also wishes to
acknowledge the Minnesota Non-Profits Assistance Fund for
its invaluable support.

New Rivers Press books are distributed by:

The Talman Company   Bookslinger
150 Fifth Avenue   2402 University Avenue West
New York, NY 10011   Saint Paul, MN 55114

Late Night Calls has been manufactured in the United States
of America for New Rivers Press, 420 N. 5th Street / Suite 910,
Minneapolis, MN 55401 in a first edition of 1,500 copies.

for my family
and for all the callers

"*. . . late at night when the Dalmane won't work*
I call the time, weather, dial-a-prayer . . .
But I know as well as you do
that there's no healing at three in the morning."

−James L. White

From the Dream Journal

Wrong Numbers

Roadside Attractions

Daydreamer

Bergy & Me

Talismans

Acknowledgements

Some of the work in this collection has appeared in the following publications, occasionally in different form: *Another Chicago Magazine, Born Again Beef* (Lost Olympics Press), *Focus Midwest, Great River Review, Greenfield Review, Laurel Review,* Moorhead State University *Advocate* and *Alumnews, Nebraska Review, New Letters, North Country, North Country Anvil, North Dakota Quarterly, Pacific Review, Poetry Now, Prairie Fire, Sidewalks, Spoon River Quarterly, Verve,* and *Wisconsin Review.*

"Fireworks" first appeared in *Stiller's Pond: New Fiction from the Upper Midwest,* © 1988 and 1991 New Rivers Press.

"The Man Who Holds the Camera" and "Celebrity Seal Found Dead" first appeared in *Stirring the Deep: The Poetry of Mark Vinz,* by Thom Tammaro © 1989 Spoon River Poetry Press.

A number of poems from this collection also appeared in *The Weird Kid* (New Rivers Press) © 1983 Mark Vinz.

Special thanks to Moorhead State University for a Faculty Release Time award, which aided in the completion of the *Late Night Calls* manuscript.

Introductory Statement

THE prose poem speaks in many voices, draws on many sources—sometimes more poetry than fiction, sometimes the reverse. A lot of people have ideas about what the prose poem is or should be, but nobody seems to know for sure. Perhaps that in itself is the joy of this particular form—one always has the sense of reinventing it as one goes along.

In general, my own guides have been Russell Edson, and Michael Benedikt's splendid anthology, *The Prose Poem;* and in particular, the work of Illinois poet Dave Etter and my fellow Minnesotans, Robert Bly and Keith Gunderson—whose prose poems are very different yet equally sustaining.

Finally, while many editors seem bewildered by the form (and their reaction is simply to avoid or ignore it), that is certainly not the case with a small group of editors whose advice and encouragement I have come to depend on: Orval Lund, Jay Meek, David Pichaske, Joe Richardson, Thom Tammaro, and Bill Truesdale. For that, I am especially grateful.

—Mark Vinz

From the Dream Journal

ANGLER

He hadn't been at it very long when he discovered that he was becoming addicted to something. It wasn't the fish, which he didn't like to handle or eat, and it wasn't the company of other fishermen, which he disliked even more. He simply had to go, and the fact that he'd never learned to swim and was still terribly afraid of drowning did not stop him from heading into deeper and deeper water each time, even though he knew there were few fish in water of that depth. For one reason or another he filed the sharp barbs off his hooks, and sometimes he forgot to put on the bait.

He knew that someday he would use up all his line, and the thought bothered him from time to time. But still he fished on alone, deeper and deeper into the dark green shadows, for he also knew that no matter how much line he let out, he would never reach bottom.

WRONG NUMBER

HE calls at midnight just to ask the time and temperature, which I give him: cold and dark. He calls at one A.M. in search of Sue. I don't know any Sues, I tell him. Well, then, how about Faye or Jean? Any girl will do. At two A.M. there is only heavy breathing and the sharp click of my dreams.

Who is this man and why has he traced me through all these years and towns, unlisted numbers and assumed names? Once he called from Honolulu just to say the surf was up. He's called from villages in the Pyrennes, a ship-to-shore from somewhere on the Great Lakes. Every place I've even wondered about, he's sure to be – that quick, familiar voice above the clots of static.

He calls me now at work and has me paged in theaters. I get to a restaurant and he's canceled the reservations. Singing telegrams. Bomb threats. Free dance lessons and opinion polls. Someday he will stop, he's told me, when I least expect it.

Four A.M. The phone rings. I must answer it now. He doesn't like to be kept waiting.

THE DREAM JOURNAL

He bought a notebook as an experiment – somewhere he read an article about dreams, about writing them down and deciphering all those strange images. That would indeed be something worth knowing – just who this other person was who lived beneath his skin. He decided to keep the journal on a table by his bed, with a small night light and a good supply of pens.

For the first two weeks his dreams were disappointing – mostly about relatives he hadn't seen in a long time, a few childhood memories, a mugger in the supermarket, and only one real nightmare about a tiger trapped in his closet. Pretty standard fare.

That was when he decided to write down the dream *first*, without the aid of sleep. He began with a giraffe which played Mozart on a flute which was its own neck, and then a great blue fish he captured and wheeled through the streets of his town on top of his machine gun calliope in the 4th of July parade. This was a definite improvement.

When he filled his notebook, he showed it to his friends, who had also been reading articles about dreams. This dream must mean that you are deeply insecure, they said, and this one clearly shows that you despise us. Alienation is becoming a real problem in your dreams, isn't it? The more they told him, the more he wrote, until they finally stopped coming to visit him and they refused to return his calls.

So he wrote on alone, and before long he began really to dream about what he had written, down to the smallest details. That was when he started mailing out his dreams – first to friends and relatives, then to newspapers and magazines. When he still didn't get any response he picked names out of the telephone directory at random. He no longer left his house more than twice a week, and all this made him strangely happy. And it made the other person – the who lived beneath his skin – even happier, though he began to whisper in that solitude between writing and sleep to try this particular dream next, or that one, like shooting the rapids in an airmail envelope, or using piranha toenail clippers. He seemed to like the frightening dreams the best, the ones about coffins and water.

He knew that someday he and the other person under his skin would have to engage in a real combat, but even this made him happy. After all, wouldn't that make a splendid dream for his journal? Soon he stopped going out at all.

WORLD CHAMPION

It started with the *Guiness Book of World Records*. He noticed that there was no category for Muzak listening, which surely must be some kind of oversight. After all, hadn't he listened to it all his life – in stores and elevators, eight hours a day at his draftsman's table, all evening on the FM? He even bought a set of headphones so he could listen in his sleep, a portable radio (also with headphones) to carry with him everywhere. Muzak was piped into every room in his house, and his swimming pool had underwater speakers. Muzak twenty-four hours a day!

He began to appear on talk shows, tiny Muzak electrode receivers embedded in his ears. "Here is your modern masterpiece," one TV host exclaimed. "Notice the smile – more enigmatic and serene than Mona Lisa's."

When his tomb was at last prepared with banks of Muzak speakers on every wall, he gave his final interview – just before the doors slammed shut. "Eternity," he said, "is one record nobody is going to beat!"

HUNTER

As the autumn hunting season draws closer, the magazines are filled with ads for guns. After days of studying the brightly colored pages, he can resist no longer. He will go out and buy a new high-powered rifle with a scope, to kill many deer he tells the clerk, who nods and grins. Notice the heavy grain of the wood, the smoothly polished stock, the hand-tooled leather sling; see how the weapon fits so snugly into the hollow of the shoulder, soft against the cheek. He also buys a box of shells, fingering their delicate weight in piles on the kitchen table, arranging them again and again into little rows of picket fences.

He rises just past midnight to oil and polish the stock and barrel once more, to test the action, the sharp and precise click of the firing mechanism. Soon he will be able to take it apart and reassemble it guided only by his fingertips.

He must find some way to fire it. Slowly he parts the bedroom curtains and raises the window and the screen. The first streaks of sunrise are breaking through the branches when the cross hairs sharpen on a small bird on the telephone pole across the street. When he squeezes the trigger, a yellow streak of fire parts the leaves and the bird explodes in a puff of feathers. How wonderful; he knew it must be like this. Nothing moves except a few headlights in the distance. This is a fine gun. It will kill many deer.

THE QUEEN GAME

THE children gather round the television set for the Miss America pageant – the Queen Game, as they call it. Who will gain the crown tonight, who will hold the winning ticket in the great dream lottery? This is the spectacle they love the best, better even than the Academy Awards or the telethon for crippled children.

Miss Arkansas gets two votes out of three. She sings off key a song from *Oklahoma*, but her hair is auburn and her mouth is full of perfect teeth. The emcee croons his spiel again, Miss California twirls a hula-hoop, Wyoming prances on a trampoline. Even the children know that talent doesn't matter here. It's all in the smile, isn't it? They watch, transfixed: Rapunzel and her golden hair, the Cinderella gown, the miller's daughter who will charm a king. And just beyond the lights and screen the cruel stepmothers gather and clap their withered hands.

A FOOT STORY

FEET are the most maligned and misunderstood parts of the human anatomy, he said: twenty-six remarkable little bones that have to bear our weight as no others. But the only time we ever think of our feet is when we stub a toe, when they are hot or tired or pinched or sprained, or when we notice how ugly they are. Hands, lips, eyes, legs, breasts and genitals, bulging biceps and flat abdomens – these are taken to be the signs of beauty by our race, he said. But who has ever written a symphony to feet?

Feet. To most they are simply a matter of odor and fungus, fallen arches and bunions, he said. But have you ever known their slender beauty? Have you ever seen a foot so delicate it took your breath away? When were feet ever seen as the emblems of rectitude or strength?

Dusky feet, he said, tiptoeing through my dreams. Lost feet bathed in cool breezes or tingling on Mediterranean sands. And the bones, he said, how wonderful the names: talus and metatarsal and calcaneus...

You sound like a fool, she said.

You ingrown nail, you stupid plantar's wart, he said, and strode off down the street – walking, of course, on his hands.

DEATH must be like a bottomless lake, he said – we sail the surface for a brief span, then sink forever.

Death must be like a fire, she said, that finally burns away all the webs and shadows, so for a moment at least we can see just what it is that has eluded us for so long. A flame eternal, like a circle – consumed and consuming, all at once.

A bottomless lake, he said.

An eternal flame, she said.

A rock, he said. Slow and imperturbable, inscrutable and cold.

A summer's day, she said, a kind of garden party where everyone will be dressed in sparkling white and everything will be perfectly still and perfectly quiet, like in a photograph.

Rubbish, he said, that's far too poetic. Which reminds me, that's what death is like, a great pile of rubbish, an eternal smoldering trash heap.

It's more like a fire engine in the night, she said. After all, what could be more fashionably poetic than your pile of rubbish? It's been done before, you know. But a red fire engine at midnight, now there's some originality. Not everyone would think of that.

I'll give you originality, he said: death is like a blinding blizzard on the plains, unstoppable, reducing all to total sameness.

Try again, she said, I saw the movie.

A bridge, he said, arching the span of years.

Really, she said, that's your problem. Such a limited imagination. No wonder you take drugs.

You're beginning to sound like a critic, he said, another case of arrested literary development.

Oh, much better, she said. There might really be some hope for you, illusory though it may seem.

I'll show you illusion, he said – garden parties and red fire engines. Damn your illusions!

Death, she said, is like a hopeless argument.

Death, he said, is like a lake, bottomless and without remorse.

THE FEAR OF LOSS

ALL his life he was afraid of something. He was always the last one out of a restaurant or theater, checking and rechecking all the seats and tables for whatever might be left behind. He opened the drawers in motel rooms, moved the furniture and beds. He made duplicates of everything he wrote, and whenever he went to the store he bought two of each item just in case one should get lost.

The older he got, the more his fear grew. His houses were filling up, he was repeating everything he said. When he became ill, he refused to see a doctor – he simply had too much to lose. When he died, deserted in the end by wives and friends, no one came to the funerals, and now, not even his children know the locations of his graves.

HOLES IN HIS UNDERWEAR

For God's sake, his mother always told him, never go out with holes in your underwear. What if you were in an accident? She was a good and dutiful mother and could be proud that he was always equipped with the best Fruit of the Loom – spotless, bleached, and even starched.

But then he went off to college and began to forget everything she had labored so long to teach him, and one day he was in a terrible car wreck. When the surgeons gathered in the Emergency Room they were amazed to find that not only was his underwear in shreds, he hadn't washed behind his ears or brushed his teeth in weeks. This would be a case for the medical journals. His poor mother was bereft. How could she face the rest of her life with the knowledge she'd failed so miserably? It was all right there in the AP press release: her name, the mother whose son was in an accident with holes in his underwear.

THE FEAR OF FAILURE

THIS is the fear that makes people feel like patriots, at least that's what my friend tells me. He's studied failure all his life, up close, until there's nothing much he doesn't know about it – like the time he dropped out of college after getting caught cheating on an exam, the time he almost got elected mayor or barely lost the big promotion at the store, the time he flunked his army physical and his cardiology report. Now he just sits on his porch and watches the traffic going past. Occasionally he's called on to give a lecture or a eulogy, but mostly he just sits. He's getting very good at it. All day long he just sits and watches and smiles.

HIS MOTHER TOLD HIM

AFTER awhile most things tend to fade and disappear, leaving if anything only a few sharp images lodged in the memory, like the pebbles in a shoe. When it came to the words of his mother, though, pebbles turned to boulders. Keep out of drafts, she always said, you'll get a chill for sure. To this day he must sleep with a cover; even on those hot and humid nights when not a single leaf is turning, he lies swaddled in bedsheets. Keep receipts, she told him, you never know just when you'll need them. His house is full of receipts, boxes of them, mountains of them. He still has the sales slip from the first pair of shoes he was allowed to purchase by himself (a pair of wingtips that pinched his toes and eventually caused him to walk duck-footed), gasoline credit slips from cars long since deceased, a canceled check from a present he bought his wife on their honeymoon – right next to the drawer of receipts for his children's braces and new bikes.

Move your bowels once a day, she said, and get eight hours of sleep; always wear galoshes in the rain, a hat in the sun. You'll get a cold, she said, you'll get the flu; your hair will fall out, you'll have a stroke. He can still hear her now, a bit more clearly every day – a voice that is thin and tired with worry, just like his own voice. And his children are watching him now, and listening, and gathering their receipts.

HISTORY LESSON

CAN you believe there was a time when people were always getting coupons in the mail for things they didn't need – like bowling lessons or dogfood – or restaurants they didn't care to try, or dry cleaners on the other side of town? History reminds us that once there were no coupon-swapping centers in every neighborhood, no coupon raffles or coupon bingo. Those were the bleak days before the formation of the National Coupon League. And can you believe they didn't even write their coupon holdings into their wills or contest them in the courts? It's a pity they didn't know that gilt-edged coupons would some day bring prime prices on the American Coupon Exchange, that every art museum would add a coupon room for the rare old master issues. Just try to imagine, if you can, what your life would be like without the gentle tones of the coupon peddlers at dusk. How would people have known who to vote for? How unutterably bare everything would have been! Though we must never forget to give credit to our forebears for discovering the coupon, we must also remember their stunning lack of foresight. History, after all, is a harsh judge, and this is but one more example of how our ancestors were indeed a curious and deficient race.

"THE Dream Riders are out there right now," she said, "just thundering in on the last light of sunset, looking for someone's dream to enter. Maybe it will be yours!"

"Like *Ghost Riders in the Sky*?" I asked, because that was Gene Autry and he was my favorite cowboy at the matinee each Saturday at the Varsity Theater.

"Definitely not like Gene Autry," she said, wrinkling up her already considerably wrinkled nose. "These riders ride long-necked giraffes and their eyes are made of gold."

"Are they chasing steers?" I asked. "Are they driving the devil's herd across an endless sky?"

"That sounds like more Gene Autry," she said. "No, they're not chasing steers, they're chasing the dreams of children."

"I thought you said they were dream *riders*," I said. "How could they be chasing dreams if they are already *in* them?"

"Listen," she said, "these are strange and ancient riders I first heard of when I was just a wee girl, and they live in a big dark forest, inside of hollow trees."

"That sounds like the Brothers Grimm," I said, because everyone knew that they told the best fairy tales, better even than the story lady on the radio.

"Listen, sonny boy," she said, and her face was all strained, "these are dream riders with giraffes and gold eyes and long whips, and they get into the dreams of children who are too smart for their own good, and I'm glad I'm not a child so I won't have to worry about those terrible Dream Riders getting into *my* dreams and filling them up with scary smoke and fire, and now you get under those covers or I'll give you another bedtime story on your backside where it just might do some good."

And that night the Dream Riders came, but they weren't riding giraffes – more like lions – and they had swords, not whips, just like in the pirate movie I went to on my birthday, and they looked like old ladies with wrinkled faces and green eyes. And when I woke up I could still smell the smoke and feel the warmth of the flames on my pillow. . .

"Just like *The Wizard of Oz*?" my daughter asks.

STATE OF THE UNION

THE face of the president hangs on the television screen like a careful portrait in oils. It is tired and guarded and the words come out in small clumps, sometimes kind and sometimes urgent, even angry. We have seen other faces like this one, many times. The words are always the same; it might be the previous president talking, or the one before him, or one before we were even born.

He speaks to us as though we were his friends, or maybe his children, as though he could see us and not the tiny red light of the camera. But he also seems to know that none of this makes any difference. It is too late for that; it has been too late for many years.

The tiny red light burns on and the portrait burns on, and when it is over nobody will be satisfied and everybody will be satisfied. For this is his duty and it is our privilege until the faces change and change again. For this is his privilege and our duty, and only the watching matters now.

FAIRY TALE

THIS is a story the children told me. It is about a happy six-year-old, who by some mistake has been put in charge of a whole classroom of stern-faced teachers – the stupidest and meanest teachers imaginable, the kind most of us have known at one time or another. First she makes them take off their shoes and their socks and stand on top of their desks, flapping their arms like crows, croaking deliriously in their wispy blue hair. Then they must sing and dance and take off the rest of their clothes – even their rings and spectacles, their wristwatches and false teeth. Last, she makes them take out everything on the *inside*, which shrivels and turns into ugly black stones. When all her students have gone outside to play, the little girl gathers the stones in her arms, carries them to the top of the highest hill, and starts them rolling. She hopes that someday they will plunge into the sea – that is, unless someone is stupid enough to stop them.

ORPHEUS REVISITED

FOR a long time he's believed that he can influence the outcome of professional football games just by moving his portable TV around the living room. Just when his team is losing he shifts the TV an inch or two, or he crosses his legs, lights a cigarette, turns on a lamp. Then everything begins to change – a dropped kick, an interception, a fumble. It's a gift, he says, a matter of constant adjustment.

That's when he gets a grave look on his face. Someday soon he'll have to go to work on basketball and golf and hockey, Wimbledon and the World Series, even the Olympic Games. Then there won't be time for anything else. It's a terrible responsibility, he says, but somebody has to do it.

SUCCESS STORY

HE couldn't remember which one went on top, Kansas or Nebraska. He stopped in Kansas once and bought a picture postcard of a grain elevator to send his great aunt in Cincinnati, or was it Cleveland? All his life he had wanted to be a traveling salesman – it didn't matter what he sold, buttons or Bibles – just the idea of having his own "territory," the thought of stopping in every small town and calling people by name. He dreamed about driving through all those vast and mysterious spaces in the heartland of his country – not the kind of driving he was used to, from his house in the suburbs to his job in the city, and back again.

So one day he headed west, all the way to Oklahoma (the one Kansas is on top of), and beyond. He tried not to think of his wife (how would she ever break the news to friends?) or their children or his great aunt. He tried not to think of anything but the flat and endless miles disappearing beneath his steel-belted radials. He would show them all, and when he had finally mapped out his own special territory, he would send back picture postcards with strange postmarks – beautiful color postcards from every stop along the way.

ANOTHER SUCCESS STORY

AFTER a particularly long night of insomnia in July, it occurred to him that sleep was probably the most wasteful commodity known to humankind. He resolved to cut back to six hours a night, then five, then four – gradually, of course, so he'd learn not to miss it. During the first month he took a second job as a night watchman. Three hours of sleep a night, then two – it was getting easier all the time, even though his loss of weight concerned his friends, as did the darkening circles beneath his eyes. He signed up for a yoga class, gave up red meat and alcohol. He was jogging now, and reading long novels.

Still, he couldn't make it through a night without nodding off, and the thought occurred to him that maybe all this was a dream, maybe he was really off somewhere in a coma. He pinched his arm: bruised flesh. The walls of his room closed in another notch. Only a few more sleepless minutes and he would win. He would take up scuba diving and pottery. He would learn to play the guitar.

A POEM THAT IS NOT PETE ROSE

THIS is the opening day of baseball season, so it's not surprising that someone like Pete Rose has got this poem caught in a rundown, and there's not much hope right now except that someone else like Pete Rose is on the steps of the dugout leading cheers, urging this poem to be robust and not to whine, urging it to slide head first – it doesn't matter that this poem's lifetime batting average is .000 and it got on base from a bean ball, and now it's scared to death that it will stumble over its own big feet. And when this poem finally slides it's like a limp belly-flop into bed, and nobody is cheering any longer.

Covered with dirt, this poem realizes again the way it's always going to be: nobody will give it a name like Doc or Catfish. This, after all, is the American pastime, where everyone is screaming for the long, hopeless slide. The best that could happen is for Pete Rose to drop the ball, but of course he doesn't. He just stands there grinning and robust, popping his bubble gum.

But here's the strange part. In spite of everything, this poem is still somehow glad it turned out his way – that it doesn't get patted on the rump very often, and that its name, after all, is not Pete Rose.

THE FEAR OF GOING DOWN

THE stillness grows heavy in the late afternoon –
everything is dripping, coated with a fine mist. Your
hand along the banister comes away wet and sticky.
The carpets and furniture lie damp and sluggish, as
if they have finally given up all hope of life.

The storm breaks without warning, shaking the
trees in one great shrug, strewing lawns with branches,
leaves, broken wires. The lightning-streaked windows
steam over, and the house becomes a diving bell slowly
rocking, miles of water crashing above it. From the
basement rise the sounds of the dead, the low moans
of many souls lost at sea for years, stirred again by the
storm.

THE EASTERN SEABOARD

It could be part of a ship, like a rudder, or maybe just an old piece of driftwood washed up on the beach, or maybe even a kind of control panel flashing green and blue lights in some dark room in, say, Greenwich, Connecticut. But some of us know that it's really a kind of game like Monopoly or Parchesi. The problem is that it frequently rains, so many of the pieces keep sliding off into the Atlantic Ocean. It's your roll again! Watch out for Atlantic City and Norfolk! I control Interstate 95 and all the hotels in Portland, Maine.

"PELLETS" is what his father had called them – strange name for rat turds – but no matter what you called them, he'd found a little trail in his dresser drawer this morning, right next to his clean underwear. He could still see his father chuckling to himself and loading the heavy traps with chunks of stale cheese. But his father was long gone, so what was he to do now? There was probably a whole family of rats in his basement, burrowing in the hollow spaces between the walls. He just knew it, even though he hadn't been able to find any other evidence. You know how rats operate!

All evening he listened for the little scraping and rustling sounds in the baseboards. All evening and half the night, and even if he heard no more than the intermittent droning of the refrigerator, he knew they were there – probably in the cupboards too, into the box of pancake flour, rat turds covering the silverware and the plates. He ate breakfast at the diner just so he wouldn't have to open any doors. "Rat pellets," he said to the waitress. She didn't seem very interested – probably had rats of her own to worry about, but not, he'd wager, a whole basement full like he had. And what about all those newspaper articles about rats attacking babies? He worried all morning about rats eating babies, and even if he didn't have any children now, someday he would. He just couldn't bear the thought of rats crawling around his kids! Rats, after all, are one of the most persistent signs of human civilization, to say nothing of all the diseases they are known to carry – bubonic plague, for instance. He was sure he wasn't immunized against that one.

He really hated to move out of his house, but with all those rats in the living room, all of those rats chewing up everything, he just couldn't see any alternatives. If he were quick about it and kept his mouth shut, maybe he could still get a decent price for his house.

FURTHER ADVENTURES OF
THE GREAT AMERICAN STORY

THE newspaper horoscope said it would be a good day for the Arts; there might be exciting messages, perhaps a residency at the Library of Congress or a new fellowship from some foundation in the Midwest. G.A.S. dusted himself off once more and ventured out onto the sunlit sidewalks in his light brown pullover. What city could this be, houses leaning together like tired parsons (his favorite line)? It wasn't the Great Plains or the Deep South – he'd been there before, but not here. No tall buildings, no ocean or desert.

He boarded the bus marked "Express" which was deserted except for a couple of shabby-looking regional poems and an autobiography in drag. "They're everywhere these days," thought G.A.S. "When will it ever end?"

They were driving toward what looked like a group of factories – tall smokestacks all around him everywhere now, and thick, black smoke. The other passengers made ugly faces and sank back into their seats. What place was this, anyway? Whatever could survive *here* but fat novels, dark and ugly and waiting to knock him down.

Toward evening the factory smoke began to clear, and he could make out a few trees. He had been dreaming again about that slim and beautiful novella he had met at the cocktail party in Manhattan, and her elusive green eyes. But now there was only the face of the driver in the rearview mirror – a sad and familiar face in the waning light.

Outside the bus windows nondescript small towns were whizzing by, turning on their lights. His horoscope had lied again. Not a good message for miles, not even a minor critic or backwater college out here. Everyone else on the bus was sleeping and soon the small cold stars would be watching him. He began to wonder if he could ever get off this bus.

HIS FATHER'S NOSE

ONE day when he looked in his shaving mirror he discovered that he had taken on his father's nose! There was no question who it belonged to – large and slightly hooked, with nostrils full of dense black hair. It was not at all like his former nose, which he had always thought fairly trim and handsome.

His wife was the first to notice the change, which was also verified by his mother and children, who were growing edgy about this stranger in the house. Soon he began to register a whole new set of smells; this nose was worthless for fine chablis or mandarin duck. Each morning he awoke to the stench of cigar smoke and canned sardines.

After much consultation with his wife and friends, it was decided that a plastic surgeon should be hired. After all, this was the kind of disaster that warranted dipping into one's life savings. But once the bandages were removed, his wife was the first to shrink back from his face. This new nose was all different again; it wasn't his father's nose, but neither was it his own. It was flatter and heavier, with a marked propensity for garlic and oysters and sea air.

The poor man visited surgeon after surgeon, each of whom tried his hand at rebuilding the nose, and soon other parts of his face – cheekbones and eyebrows and lips. And after awhile, when the savings were spent and his wife and children had taken up residence in another state, not one of the people who once knew him could recognize his face. No one, that is, except his mother, who knew that even if her side of the family had contributed the weak jaw and tiny ears, he still possessed his father's hands, his father's slouch and gait, his father's deep-set and unmistakable eyes.

VOCATION

THERE was a time he was content memorizing the Periodic Table of Elements. He received great sustenance from knowing that W is the symbol for Tungsten, Md for Mendelevium. It was also quite useful for crossword puzzles.

Then, for no explainable reason, his life began to shift. He read some books. He began keeping a journal. He found a support group of other people whose lives had inexplicably shifted and who were also keeping journals. He kept on writing and shifting and taking long walks by himself. Everything seemed to catch his attention. Sometimes he made it through an entire Sunday afternoon without turning on the TV set.

Perhaps, he thought, he should go away by himself – to a place he could let all his hair grow, a place he could go barefoot and wear serapes if he chose. It would have to be far away from what he was used to – out in the Midwest, maybe – somewhere he could find the solitude he craved, somewhere he could find a job teaching creative writing.

THE LAST WORD

His writing hadn't been going very well – only a few scant poems, a few clumsy short stories, and a great stack of rejection slips. He was, of course, drinking heavily, and his friends grew increasingly concerned. One of them, trying to find some way to cheer him up, brought over an old quill pen he had found in the attic of the house he rented. Who knows, he said, this could even be the writing instrument of some great author from the past.

At the end of a particularly dreary week of writing, and half drunk, he decided to try the quill. It was awkward in his hand and scratchy on the page, but there was also a new feeling, a kind of mild exhilaration – perhaps because what he was doing seemed so ludicrous. But when he looked closely at the jagged words in front of him there was indeed some indefinable quality that had not been there before.

He experimented with the quill more and more each day, and with a variety of colors of ink. He decided he liked red the best – red, like his own spent blood. Why not blood itself, then? Carefully, he cut into the end of his left forefinger and from the tiny pool of blood on his desk he began to write a poem. It grew longer; he had to re-open the wound several times to finish the draft, then the revisions. But when the poem was done it was truly the best thing he had ever written, and indeed, it was soon accepted for publication by a small magazine in the Midwest.

He wrote more and more. The friend who brought him the quill pen also happened to work in a hospital, so they made secret arrangements to have a pint of his blood drawn each week, then two pints. He was working on a novel – a great novel – and when they found him in his room one morning lying dead in a pool of his own blood, only his friend from the hospital could guess the reason he had died. He gathered the manuscript pages from the dead writer's desk, took them home, and read late into the night. What he could make out was very good, but there were too many blotches and indecipherable passages, too many places where the words seemed literally to crumble off the pages. It was hopeless.

He looked one last time at the pile of pages, the thin scrawl of his poor friend's handwriting, and then he smiled. He would slip the manuscript into the coffin. That would be a fitting end to the whole bizarre episode. When he thought about it, though, the whole thing just might make a good short story. He had always secretly thought about doing some writing. He would have to try his hand at it.

Wrong Numbers

THE MUZAKS

"Our submission seems required by public ugliness in our critics, by the public nonsense of television which threatens to turn our brains into farina within our heads, by even such trifling things as Muzak broadcasts in the elevators of public buildings."

— Saul Bellow

BACH or Beach Boys, Beatles or Berlin – they all sound the same. But that's just what we want, isn't it? What relaxes us, increases our production, fills some deep need for background. It's the laugh track for elevators, the have-a-nice-day message when we're put on hold, the vibrator bed we can take anywhere. Who are these people, anyway. . .whose spoor we read in every TV speech and sitcom, in every ad, in every glottal stop?. . .

Somewhere beyond the newest subdivisions wait the spawning pools. From deep beneath the glucose scum the tiny bubbles rise, in each a violin refrain, a glob of technicolor, or a purgatorial smile – rising and popping, rising and popping, and hovering in steamy waves.

AT BETTER STORES EVERYWHERE

"Last year, American parents spent over one billion dollars on lifelike war toys for their children."

– Paul Harvey

WE call it Survival Town, a realistically detailed miniature village which can be modified to suit various locales – complete with assorted huts and villagers, school and church, hillside honeycombed with tunnels which Dad and the kids will love to find new ways to booby-trap, 2 tanks, and 3 helicopters for the assault troops: 32 miniature personnel in full camouflage gear (all model weaponry certified state of the art). Completely portable – folds up neatly in its own carrying case, with all parts made of durable, high-impact plastic for years of reuse. Batteries and explosives not included.

PROGRESS REPORT

"She wondered why horror movies had to be remade – maybe because the world was getting scarier all the time."

— Bobbie Ann Mason

IT used to be so simple – bad lighting and a stormy night, a few frightened villagers, the certainty that everything would be back in its dusty coffin before the lights came up. Sure, the Old World scared us but we always beat it back, burned its crumbly castles, laughed up our sleeves at its outrageous acting. Some things, you know, are best left to God. We foolish humans never learn. Good stuff.

Then came the plastic suits – you had to look hard not to see the seams. Tokyo flamed and we learned to cheer the monsters all over again, the aliens among us, the evil galaxies next door. The new world is still the old one, but Science triumphs now, not God.

And the villagers? They're still afraid to go outside at night, of course – even now they gather in their houses whispering of all the terrifying things that lurk beyond their walls. Stay tuned for bulletins. Late news on your local stations, followed by special reports.

CELEBRITY SEAL FOUND DEAD

THAT'S what the headline from the AP wire story says, but someone has cut out the rest of the page, so there's no story. But what's there to tell, really? It's all too familiar by now – another victim of controlled substances, fishy binges in New York and LA, the same tired screed of slippery accusations. He worked for small fry when he should have ruled the tank, and then one day even Dave and Johnny stopped calling. They claimed he just didn't give a toot anymore. *Enquirer* claimed he'd been seen with sharks in dives. *He* claimed he was cleaning up his act, learning some new tunes, barking up another tree – so what if his career was on the rocks, he'd resurface soon. . . . That's when they found him, whisker-down in the pool. You can imagine the rest – small wake, sealed coffin, the mysterious porpoise in black. It's all too familiar.

So watch for the book and the made-for-TV movie out this fall. And remember this: a lot of us mammals love the clapping too much for our own good. Who can really blame him for getting tired of shelling out? Face it, he was a showman – right to the salty end, all the way to the unfathomable bottom.

YOMPHEADS

Goose and Harley are driving around looking for a bait shop, reading the bumper stickers in every parking lot: FOXY GRANDMA, JESUS IS THE ONE, HAVE YOU HUGGED A WELDOR TODAY? and WORK IS FOR PEOPLE WHO DON'T FISH.

"That's the one you should get you," says Harley, dumping the car ashtray in front of the Dairy Queen. "Help to hold your bumper on."

"What I should get me," says Goose, sucking his Slurpy like a sump pump, "is a new car, period. Get me one of them for'n cars like everybody else."

"Why not?" says Harley, grinning snoose down his chin. "You already got you a for'n rod 'n reel, a for'n chainsaw, and a for'n TV."

"Get me a for'n wife, too, and some for'n kids. A for'n mama and a big for'n house," says Goose, cracking the dashboard with his fist.

"What say we forget about that bait?" says Harley. "Go out to County 6 and do us a target shoot."

"They put up some new road signs?" says Goose.

"You bet," says Harley, "and if you head us back to the trailer for the rifles we go right by Archie's hardware place."

"Hot dogs and Pepsi 10 cents on Saturday?" says Goose.

"You bet," says Harley.

"Hot damn," says Goose, swinging the '68 LeSabre toward the sinking sun. "You sure do know what a fella really needs."

"HAVE you heard the news?" asks Clover. "They've opened a K-Mart Medical out in the Village Green Mall."

"Heard it a long time ago," says Milly. "Mrs. Gumlow up the street already went in for gall bladder. Blue Light Special on gall bladders last week, you know."

"How about the kidney stones and ankle swell?" asks Clover.

"Shouldn't be long now, I'd reckon," says Milly. "The new ad comes out in Thursday's paper. Been thinking about getting my hip fixed, too, but Estelle tells me they'll be running two-fers around the end of the month."

"That Estelle," says Clover. "She always was one to go right up and ask."

"How else are you going to find out?" says Milly. "We should probably give them a call ourselves. Jessie's youngest boy is having sore tonsils again, you know. Maybe I can get him a gift certificate for Christmas."

"Make a swell stocking-stuffer," says Clover. "Maybe I can get Ed's back looked at, too. What if we just jumped in the Pinto and drove over town? Never know about those Blue Light Specials, you know. No telling what we'll find when we get out there."

"Slow down, honey," says Milly. "I'll get my hat."

ROUGH FISH

WE'RE trying to get them out of the lake, the game warden says – carp, suckers, buffalo fish. It's no wonder, either. You can only guess what they're doing down there – butting heads, swapping filthy stories, comparing tattoos. Haven't you heard them? They're out there in the shallows every evening, gorging themselves like hooligans, thrashing and laughing all night long.

DEPARTMENT MEETING

In the elegant ballroom the duelists salute each other, sabers flashing in the light from chandeliers. Behind them, all the lords and ladies watch in small clusters, whispering among themselves. Parry, thrust, and counter-thrust, the duelists move as one, neither gaining nor falling back. Someone stifles a yawn. Another walks out to the veranda for a breath of air as a new pair of duelists replaces the first, and then another. Lunge and touch, feint and glide – a chorus of sighs rises, and suddenly the parquet floor is covered with duelists, each pair lost to every other. Nothing matters now beyond the shine and clank of blades, the masked duelists moving as one against each other in ever-shifting circles. Nothing matters at all.

"A TEACHER, eh? So whaddya teach?" the man on the next barstool asks.

"English," I say, trying to look nonchalant.

"Never was any good in English," he says, scanning me as if I were a fireplug. "Hated all them damn papers."

That's what they all say, afraid to speak any more in case I might want to correct them, grade their style and usage, nail a few dead metaphors to the wall. Conan the Grammarian. Me Red Felt-tip, You Comma Splice.

"It's not like that," I say, scratching my belly and slurring my vowels. Too late, he's already heading toward the cranberry slack convention in the corner booth for some plain talk about ball scores, weather, and uppity women.

"It's a dirty job," I say to the bartender, "but somebody has to work for tenure."

"You sound like a T-shirt," he says.

"Whaddya mean?" I say, trying to squint like a longshoreman. "Who do you think I am, anyway?"

"Whom," he says. "Objective case of the pronoun. May I bring you another drink?"

"English major?" I say.

"You bet your dangling participle," he says. "Seen any promiscuous syntax lately?"

There we sit till closing, grinning like sentence fragments, practicing our secret grips.

THE FAMOUS AUTHOR

HE came to town last week to read his work to an overflow crowd in the college auditorium. Isn't it remarkable, we all said, the way he looks just like his photographs – puckish grin and shock of silver hair, sleek and charming in his double-breasted suit. Just look at him posing shyly for the cameras, which are suddenly everywhere. There's even a camera lens poking through the curtains behind him on the stage as he reads, clicking again and again – pictures of the famous author's backside, pictures of the audience smiling contentedly as the famous author gives them a long, long story that nobody seems to follow.

And then, the famous author has a plane to catch – but not before he puts his hand and footprints in the wet cement prepared for him on the Walk of Fame downtown. It's not often we get such celebrities – just ask the local anchorman watching with his microphone. Isn't it remarkable, he nods, reading aloud the name the famous author has written with a Popsicle stick on the drying sidewalk. Tell me again just what it is he writes, the anchorman says, as far above us in the charming, photogenic clouds the famous author jets away to another town.

THE phone rings at 8 A.M., just as I am stumbling toward the bathroom. "I'm a nationally published writer," the voice says, "but I've got some questions about first North American serial rights."

Half an hour later the phone rings again, just as I'm sitting down with coffee and ball scores. "What do you feel about free verse?" I'm asked. "Who have you been reading?" I say – too late, by now I should know better. "Well," comes the reply, "I try not to read at all. That way I won't get influenced."

Who keeps giving these people my name? The 9:15 caller wants to know about personal journals. 9:30 asks about cover letters and comma rules, and 10:00 informs me, "I'm sure you'd like to read my new novella. It's right up your alley."

Just what is my alley? Regionalism? The 10:25 caller wants to know about regionalism and the quest for a definitive idiom. "It's Saturday," I say. "I never discuss idiom on weekends." "Well," says the caller, "that's not what I've heard."

So I'm a liar. My basement is filling up with manuscripts and unanswered mail. If it weren't for my family, I'd rip the phone off the wall. "I need to know how to get my book out" interrupts my lunch. "When I send it to a publisher, how much will they pay me and how soon?"

I hide out in bars for the rest of the day. "Been

thinking," says the fat man on the next stool, "it's time I sat down and wrote about my life. My kids have told me that for years. What do you think?" "Have another beer," I say. "How about those Vikings? Do you think beet prices will drop? Did you hear about the latest bombing in Beirut?"

Midnight bugs smash themselves against my screens. Larry hits Moe, Curly hits the wall. "Tell me," says the voice on the phone, "what do you recommend for writer's block?"

REJECTION SLIPS

He couldn't remember how many he'd collected – he gave up counting after papering two bedrooms and a half-bath. Once they had driven him to the point of a breakdown, but now he really didn't mind them. After all, like the obit page and the irs, they were something you could count on, and he had to admit that he needed something to count on.

Dear Doctor _____:

We're sorry to report your diagnosis is not suited to our present needs. But thank you for submitting it. We're sure you'll place it elsewhere.

Some days he was philosophical. He could even look at the whole process as contributing to the national economy. Someone had to compose those messages after all. Someone had to print them, put them in the return envelopes, sort them, fly them from city to city, and deliver them.

Dear Senator _____:

You're very strong on dialogue and description, but your plot seems too far-fetched to resolve the conflicts. We'd like to suggest you pay more attention to character development. Good luck.

One thing he could always pride himself on was taking their suggestions – the few that were offered anyway. He'd even attended night school for awhile, joined a writer's support group, re-read the classics.

Dear Professor _____:

Have you considered getting to know your audience better? What you offer comes very close for us, but finally we feel it lacks the insight we're looking for. Keep trying. We're always open to new submissions.

He'd even gone back and examined the reasons for doing it all in the first place. Did he really show promise? Was he just a hopeless optimist? Had *he* invented the rules, things might have been different – but when it came right down to it, all he could really do was keep on playing the game.

Dear Reverend _____:

After careful consideration, we regret to say your work is not quite right for us. There's much fine sound and fury here, but we're not sure what it signifies. Perhaps you need to give some more thought to your ending.

THE EDITOR

MOSTLY he dreams about all the letters he should have written last month, and now everything is lost – he's looked everywhere, every drawer and wastebasket, over and over. There will be lawsuits. They're going to take him to trial without his serial rights.

Sometimes he dreams he's dead. This time it's from poisoned glue. Small men in trenchcoats creep out from beneath the bed and begin to strip the body. Just as we suspected, they say – once you get beneath the wrappers, there's not much there at all.

He lies in bed, sweating, listening to the birds outside his window. A little flat on the low notes, but not bad for a regional effort. A car stops out front, then quick footsteps up the walk, and the mail slot clinks. He lies in bed sweating, trying to remember what he's done with the children, wondering just what it is that is going to explode next.

A THEORY OF POETRY

TODAY for some reason, I think about a man I knew a long time ago, his beautiful wife and their baby – a boy or girl, I can't remember, only that they fed it paregoric so it wouldn't cry or fuss. That's the way a baby should be, they said, when both parents are poets, when they have visitors and need to talk. The morning was perfect: we drank mulled wine and spoke of Yeats and Joyce and Paris in the Twenties, then ate gazpacho in the cool, lacy shadows of the little arbor.

Not long after that day, the man and his beautiful wife were divorced – he for at least the third time. Certainly it was painful, he told me, but he'd gotten a lot of good poems out of that marriage, and didn't that make it worthwhile after all? All I could think of were the deep brown eyes of the baby in the bassinet, looking up, past me, far away.

I can't begin to say how many poems I've read since then, in how many places. Sometimes one of them will call me back and I'll remember that morning, the man and his wife sipping wine beside the sleeping baby. But not even once do I remember reading the man's name.

THE CHAIN LETTER

IT arrives with no return address, of course – promising good fortune, new friends. It's a chain that's been around the world several times, it says. To break it will surely bring bad luck, even disaster. Only a fool would consider breaking the chain. There are stories of what might happen to fools.

Ridiculous, you tell yourself, to believe such nonsense. Who could have done this to you? Half the morning you wonder, and then you address the first envelopes – to your supervisor, to *his* supervisor, all the way up. Foolish to risk the curse of broken chains? Who can really say?

There will, of course, be repercussions. Memos from above, new policies, more memos. Half the morning you wonder what they'll wonder, checking and rechecking your list. You wonder, too, if all this will ever come back to you. You wonder what you're going to learn – about chains, about luck, about fools.

WORLD ENOUGH, AND TIME

WATCHES. The man at the hardware counter wears a black one sprouting dials and gauges. The clerks at the department store are modishly digital. The biker at the Auto-Teller scans a dented pocket piece he's slipped out from a maze of leather jacket zippers. Even the beautiful model lolling by the ocean on the swimsuit billboard wears one – a slim gold bracelet set off against yards of bronze skin.

The kids destroyed mine years ago – my high school graduation present, whose dial steamed up in any weather. I never got a replacement, just the old Bulova my mother found in some parking lot. Everybody needs a watch, you know – I keep mine in a clay pot with all the other odds and ends I don't quite know what to do with. It's in there now, still ticking, since I had to wear it yesterday to give a speech, and even so, I went on longer than I should have. That's the problem, you know – some of us still haven't learned to tell time.

We're the ones you have to look out for – stubborn throwbacks to an age when things weren't so organized. That's what we like to believe, anyway. And so what if we're irritating? Who else can make you feel so good about your own punctuality? See? I've probably gone on too long again. What a grinning fool I must be. Doesn't that make you feel better already?

WIND CHILL

THE voice on the radio is urgent. When you go out-side, it says, exposed flesh will freeze in less than a minute. Minus sixty-five this morning, and it will get worse through the daylight hours – who knows how much worse when the wind comes up, when it really comes up. Records will fall. Can't you feel it, there in the dim light of the kitchen, small drafts creeping through every pore? Think of flesh, the voice whispers. Think of bare flesh, numbing, tightening. Think of records, what you'll tell the others, the ones who don't live here, the ones who'll never understand. Listen, says the fading voice: this is what we believe in. Listen: this is everything we know.

BLIZZARD FOOD

It starts with chips and soda pop, then spreads in all directions. Should be quite a storm, we say in every aisle. Should be getting here any time now – we heard the forecast on TV.

What are we going to do? The shelves are emptying fast. You've got to buy everything, you see. You've got to stock up. And now there aren't enough shopping carts to go around. Everyone in town is coming through those automatic doors, crashing into each other in the check-out lanes, while outside, cars are being rammed in the parking lot as shoppers try to get away to other stores. Who can blame them? Even if it never lasts more than a day or two, you simply *have* to stock up. After all, you never know what you're going to need in a blizzard.

ROCKS

It amazed him what some people could do with them – build walls, make sculptures, discover fossils. Whole books had been written on rocks, and somewhere, he was sure, there was even a novelist at work on the theme of rocks.

He, on the other hand, had no real knowledge of rocks. He kept a few on his window sill – souvenirs from trips to Lake Superior or the desert – but he didn't even know their names. Just rocks, fascinating rocks, sparkling in sunlight through the curtains or just sitting there, dark and mysterious. Perhaps some ancient tribe had fingered one of those rocks.

When he tried to talk to his wife about rocks, she always had the same reply. "Rockhead," she said, "don't talk to me until you have something to say." She didn't seem to care that whole civilizations had revolved around rocks.

There they sat on the window sill, a few scattered specimens – all she'd let him bring into the house. Every now and then he'd turn them over in his hands, just to feel their weights and textures. How simple they were, how they possessed him.

His wife was right, you know.

FAMILY ALBUM

THE bureau drawers are full – what else do you do with them? Line them up in little frames on the TV? Fill the walls? Make albums? Even if that's what we wanted, there are far too many – mine, yours, theirs, boxes in the basement, shelves of dusty slide trays, the faces we can't quite place and even some we can. Who's that fat kid in the cowboy suit, those little girls on the swingset? Cousin What's-his-name with his new Buick – now there's a revealing pose. What year was that? And look at all those fish we caught – if only the light had been better – the candid shot of Mother in her flapper dress, and Great Aunt So-and-so's wedding picture back at the farm in Wisconsin, or was it Dakota? Why didn't they write something on the back? Let's just throw them in a bigger box for now – we'll find a place. But someday soon we'll have to do some serious sorting. Write that down. One of those vacation weekends. One of those rainy days when we're all in the mood.

LONG DISTANCE

You call again tonight to say the old days are all gone –
how long has it been? How long?

What holds us now is surely less than it was then –
the thread of years unraveling with questions neither
one of us can answer anymore.

What time is it? Beyond these lines is sleep, our
lives the rooms we step from, closing doors. Across
the wires a pulse of static, other voices breaking in,
breaking up. It's getting late. Next time, *I'll* call – an easy
promise between old friends, wondering just what it
is that holds them past these voices straining in their
ears.

DISAPPEARING ACT

FIRST, you have to remember Sinclair gasoline, that green brontosaurus logo – gone the way of Burma Shave signs, I suppose. But not quite, at least not when we stopped at the Sinclair Lewis Interpretive Center just outside of Sauk Centre, Minnesota, followed by a family from a listing Winnebago in the parking lot. Mom, Dad, and the three kids streaming through the place, where all they could find was stuff about some dead guy, some writer. "Where's the dinosaur?" Mom kept saying. "I thought this was about a dinosaur." Then they were off to the Interstate again, disgusted, I suppose, at losing time. And I stood awhile among the old photographs, wondering about memorabilia, wondering about dinosaurs, and what I'd be meeting on the road ahead.

CLASS REUNION

ACCORDING to the directory, most of us are in accounting, sales, or law. The odd are odder, loud louder, and aside from missing hair the jocks have held up pretty well; the organizers organize, the wall flowers have found a mission in their homes and kids. What surprises is the few surprises. We've even died the way we should, in car wrecks, cancer ward and jungle wars, divorced occasionally, been broadened through our travels, taken up aerobics, jogging, golf. Everybody's happy here, and doing well.

So here we sit in those tight groups defined so many years ago, waiting again for someone to drink too much or spark some long-forgotten feud, wondering which cars out there are the rented ones, whose spouses are secretly desperate. Stories rise and fall like summer breezes, as we try to remember just what it is we don't remember. So good to see you, glad we've come, let's keep in touch – and quickly, now, let's get away from here, drink up. That's it – let's make our escape. Again.

TRUE BELIEVER

Sure, they're slumping again, seems like they're always slumping, their last one's stretched for fifteen seasons, but this year we've got the talent, you know, we've got the hitters – long ball hitters, spray hitters, opposite field hitters, pinch hitters, clutch hitters. The pitching has to come around, you know – the pitching and the fielding, the base stealing and the managing. We've started a pool on the manager, you know – he might last through the week, but we're betting not. There'll be another manager soon, that's all we really need – they're lining up in the press box, they're lining up in the locker room, in the TV booth, in the concession stands, waiting, their overnight bags all packed, practicing their moves, practicing their spitting. We're coming back, you know, just wait till the All-Star break, just wait till the second half, we'll be there at the end, you'll see – when we solidify the starting rotation and the defense, the base stealing and the bullpen, you'll see, and we can't forget the manager. I'm counting on Tuesday – how about you?

THE COACH'S CHILDREN

Just after midnight I wake up to shouts and a strange thumping sound. The coach who lives next door is outside in his dimly lighted driveway, shooting baskets with his children. They are running pattern drills, all five of them – the coach, his three teenage sons, and his ten-year-old daughter.

I hate to complain to good neighbors, but tomorrow is a work day and I need my sleep. Trying to keep quiet so I won't wake my wife, I fumble in the dark for clothes – sneakers, jeans, an old sweatshirt. It must be near freezing tonight. There have already been some hard frosts, so at least most of the bugs are gone – just shadows and children beneath the moon's thin smile. Rebound! they scream in unison as the ball rims toward me – dribble, pass, and get in line. Hustle-up, baldy, the little girl tells me as I watch her layup cut the net. My hands are numb. I haven't held a ball in years. Hustle-up, the coach shouts behind me, the red arc of a cigarette disappearing into the bushes. We're running faster now, cutting and weaving and popping them in from the top of the key, scarcely noticing lights coming on all over the neighborhood – only the ball, the blur of hands and breath, the empty basket waiting.

MESSAGE

THE old man around the corner used to come out and yell at the children when they walked the dog. Keep away from my yard, he'd say – if you know what's good for you. Now, our dog is dead, and the old man is so crippled up he can't even come outside.

The old man up the street used to ride his bike every evening, his dog trailing behind on a long leash. When the dog finally died, the old man quit riding his bike. A few months later, wandering alone in the street by the post office, the old man was hit by a car.

On my walk home from the store I meet another old man, cradling his small dog in his arms. She's too crippled up to walk by herself, he tells me – but she sure loves to get outside every day.

Maybe we should get another dog, my wife tells me – now that the children are grown up. Everywhere I walk today, I hear barking – from houses, backyards, passing cars. Keep away, if you know what's good for you. Behind every window, there's an old man, watching.

HIS RECENT BREAKDOWN

1. *Major Repairs*

A MAN is driving to the post office to buy a stamp, when suddenly the engine of his Fairlane starts to clatter like an insane sewing machine. Valves, says the mechanic at the Texaco station. Your valves are shot.

My valves are shot, the man says sadly to his wife when he finally returns home.

It's no wonder, says his wife. Look at what you've been eating.

2. *The Sleep Lesson*

You were snoring again, he says.

I don't snore, she says.

How do you know, he says, if you're asleep when you do it?

Because, if I were snoring, I'd wake myself up.

Well, you woke *me* up with your snoring, he says.

And you're the one who woke *me* up, she says, which probably means you're the one who was snoring in the first place. Men snore more than women, you know. You woke yourself up with your own snoring and then you had to wake me up because you were awake.

If you're so smart, he says, then tell me how long this has been going on.

Ever since you started talking in your sleep, she says.

I don't talk in my sleep, he says. If I did, then according to your logic, I'd wake myself up.

Don't be silly, she says. Your sleep talking is far too boring to wake anybody up.

Tell me, he says, how long has it been like this?

3. *Long Distance*

A MAN and his wife are sitting in the living room after their evening meal, when the phone rings. The woman answers because her chair is closest to the phone.

Who was it? the man asks.

Your best friend, she replies.

Then why didn't you let me speak to him?

He was in far too good a mood to talk to you, she says.

Shouldn't I be able to decide that? he says.

That depends, she says.

On what? he says.

On whether you're a better judge of moods than friends.

4. *The Conspiracy*

A MAN is being served a bowl of stew by his wife. As he eats, he discovers several long hairs in his stew. That's disgusting, the man says.

I knew I should have used more bay leaves, says his wife.

When the man sits down after supper, there is hair all over his favorite chair, hair on his newspaper, hair in his tobacco.

The world is coming unstuck, says the man.

Gesundheit! says his wife, picking at a hair floating in her cup of coffee.

As the man showers before bed, the drain clogs up. He fishes out a wad of hair just as the tub is about to overflow.

This must be some kind of conspiracy, the man shouts to his wife.

You look ridiculous, she says. Go upstairs and put on some clothes.

THE BLUE STUFF IN THE TOILET

Don't use the toilet, she said. I'm cleaning it.

With that blue stuff? he said.

Of course, she said. There's blue stuff in the toilet, so don't use it.

Why must you always put that blue stuff in the toilet just when I have to use it?

You'd never understand, she said. Some things aren't meant for you to understand.

That night when he woke up at 3 A.M. he heard a low chuckling coming from the closet. Everyone, he sighed, understands about that blue stuff, everyone but me.

FATHER'S HOME

HE paused on the stairs. Even though he was quite sure everyone was asleep, there were voices coming from every bedroom. His wife was conducting some kind of meeting. "Coffee anyone?" she was saying. "We need a motion on the next amendment."

One of his children was moaning in a low, steady voice. Another was laughing, the third singing – the melody was familiar though he couldn't make out the words.

He turned and headed back toward the landing, knowing it would be awhile yet before he could get to sleep. His family constantly bewildered him – the way someone was always in the bathroom just when he needed it, the way they were always late when he was ready and ready when he was late, the way the phone was always busy whenever he called home. "I tried to call home for nearly three hours today," he'd say, but his wife always had the same response: "Well, I don't know what number you were calling. Nobody here was on the phone all day long, at least not for more than five minutes at a time. Are you sure you were calling the right number?"

He stood on the landing looking out the window at the moonlight on the snowdrifts in the back yard. Everything was covered with eerie light. He stared out the window for a long time, listening to the voices above him and imagining that he and his family were outside playing in the snow in the moonlight. They were building a giant snowman, laughing and singing and rolling in the snow. Then he heard the toilet flush and decided to go back downstairs to the kitchen table, where he sat in the dark sipping a glass of milk.

Whenever he came home from work, he'd hear his wife yell out, "Your father's home." Then there would be a great deal of scurrying and bustling about, and when he walked into the living room, there they'd be — quiet, neat, expectant.

"How was your day?" he'd ask.

"Oh, the usual," his wife would say.

"Same old stuff," the three children would say. "But we've been keeping busy."

He moved his hands in and out of the patches of moonlight on the kitchen table, watching them change color in the glow. The furnace started up – his furnace, his table, his house. It made him feel substantial.

Back on the quiet stairway landing he took one last look out the window. He would have to remember to tell his family about the moonlight on the snow.

As he turned to climb the rest of the stairs, he heard his wife's voice from the bedroom. "Your father's home," she was saying. "Get ready, your father's home."

Roadside Attractions

QUESTION

I HAVEN'T been back for years, he says, meaning his hometown, which is out there somewhere beyond the sweep of his arm – not quite forgotten, one of those places it's all right to come from, but who would ever go back there for very long, and what would there be to *do?* Maybe that should be an end to it, though there's a sadness in his voice and a kind of secrecy, as if he's about to say something about how it was to live there – some special thing he remembers, like a neighbor's green apple tree. And what *did* the post office look like, and when did they tear down the theater? And it's too bad that Mrs. So-and-so died, even if she was a very old lady. Maybe that's what he wants – to come back to that old hometown years later, slightly famous or simply tired, and somebody there will know him and be glad he's come back, even though it's just for a little while. And yes, he'll say, it's good to be back *home* again, and the word is strange in a way he hadn't realized. Maybe he's traveled farther than he thought, and if this really isn't home, what is?

STILL LIFE: A GOOD ALL-NIGHT CAFE

THE waitresses are high school girls wearing their boy-friends' graduation rings on chains around their necks. They stand together at the end of the counter, talking about the new movie at the drive-in and the good friends who have moved away.

Only a few customers now – a family that just pulled in from the highway for coffee and cokes to go, two truck drivers dozing in the corner booth, and three old ladies wearing hats and gloves who have just come from the weekly bridge game. Soon the bars will close and a few people will probably stop for breakfast on their way home.

The manager sits in his little office back by the restrooms. No good reason anymore to keep the place open all night – but he'd hate to hit a town like this and not find a cafe open. He still serves a fine cup of coffee. That's the secret: keep the counters clean, make sure the coffee pot is always on. Maybe things will pick up next week.

STILL LIFE: THE PLEASURES OF HOME

THE locusts are back this year, and toward sunset the racket is beyond all toleration – like a giant bandsaw hidden in the tops of the elm trees. But soon it will be dark and there will be a few hours of silence again, broken only by the hiss of tires, a porch door slamming, a barking dog.

The humidity is back again too, the worst this summer it's ever been, worse than any of the old men can remember. There's a dull ring around the streetlight, so heavy it seems to be dripping, as the front porches slowly fill up with people and paper fans. The old women come out after putting away the dishes, and sit in metal lawn chairs, their legs far apart, their stockings rolled down below their knees. The front room windows are streaked with blue and white light from the TV sets, and now and then the angry voice of a child calls out from within the house.

Everyone is thinking about sleep, about damp, sticky sheets. Something seems to be stirring out there in the dark fields. Heat lightning to the south. Perhaps tonight there will be a breeze.

STILL LIFE: BARBER SHOP IN A SMALL TOWN

THE shop is full of men today – a few in business suits and a few in overalls, reading newspapers or magazines or simply staring out at the cars and people moving through the town square. Once in a while someone will comment on the humidity or the price of gas, and everyone nods and smiles. If they wanted to, they all could call each other by their first names.

Some of the men have close-cropped hair; as though they just had haircuts but have come back today because they don't know what else to do. In fact, nobody has long hair; there are no beards or mustaches, only a few ragged edges around sunburned necks. The two barbers are talking back and forth about fishing. After work they are going to the river just below the dam. They will catch only carp and other rough fish, but it won't matter. When you're not in a barber shop, a river is a good place to be.

The barber cloth snaps and the next customer rises and stretches and moves toward the empty chair. The low hum of clippers swims through turning pages, the little puffs of talcum powder hanging in the air.

STILL LIFE: BELOW ZERO

THIS is the time when everything has been put away – the last weeks of winter when the terrible sameness of days lines up like jars of preserves in the cellar. The best ones, the fresh and surprising ones, are gone. All that remains are those that were slid down to the end of the shelf, with no variation except in degree – just more of the same, and more. Winter never saves the best for last, and today it's below zero again, for the fiftieth or sixtieth time. No one keeps count, no one needs to be told just how cold it really is. Even the words freeze up.

The houses look tired and indifferent under the gray sky, the children's abandoned snow fort, the footprints drifting over one more time. The husband sits in front of the TV set watching a soap opera. In the kitchen the wife clucks quietly to herself over the drooping geraniums above the sink. Next year they must find a means to go away, far away, to the place of postcards, so far away they will even begin to miss the snow, the hungry icicles hanging from the eaves, the slow breath of the almost empty house.

GARDENER

HE had lived in this place for a very long time, long enough to see the coming and going of many gardens. All his children had grown up and moved away, but he was still thankful he'd been able to keep the small house at the edge of town – where he had almost as many books as vegetables. Sometimes he looked around him and tried to imagine his house in some small country town in Wales or Ireland. If he squinted his eyes just right he could almost see some old vicar on a bicycle meandering down a country lane flanked by stone fences. He'd never been very far from home, and even though his children were very good about writing him from all the places they lived or visited, he didn't have much desire to leave – especially not during growing season. Along the top of the mantel he lined up the picture postcards from a score of different places, many with strange and exotic names.

This would be another good year for sweet corn, and already the squash and cucumber blossoms loaded the thick vines. Deep in their burrows the carrots and onions and radishes sent down their tiny roots. Beans and tomatoes hung tight and green. He stood in the middle of the garden plot – sometimes he even hated to pull the weeds, so alive and fibrous. He never could get the stain off his hands.

Soon enough it would be time to put all the vegetables up in mason jars again, whatever he couldn't eat or give away. There was always so much, and the jars lined the cellar shelves, row after row. But then, he never knew when one of the children might show up for a visit. He worked in the garden all day and part of the evening too. There would be time for books when the snow came.

He squinted his eyes against the sun and imagined that down the road he saw a procession of gypsy wagons, blue and green and red. This would be another fine crop – he would write everybody and tell them what a good crop it was this year. He squinted his eyes again and saw his children coming down the road, silently in single file. Their faces were smiling and bright, like blossoms, and their long, wild hair billowed out behind them in the sudden summer wind.

TRAVELING TOWARD HOME

Driving through the Dakotas at night, a man and his wife are suddenly stopped by a road construction crew, leaping around in the dust like Sunday school boys at a picnic. A workman with a flashlight waves them onto a gravel road that disappears into a wheatfield. Soon the glow from the giant earthmoving machines fades from the rearview mirror.

After half an hour, the woman finally asks where they are. Another detour, the husband says. It's getting darker, the woman says, as they both peer out of the dusty car windows, straining to follow the beam of the headlights, the roads that follow each other around in the night. There must be thousands of them — asphalt, gravel, dirt, ruts, crisscrossing the land like a nerve network that might take them places they don't want to go. They never could follow all those roads, could they? All those roads across the prairie, where here and there a light blinks on far away, miles and miles away.

LEAF-WATCHER

EACH fall a man and his family take a trip to look at the changing leaves. It always seems they're just a few days late – so many of the trees are already bare, and didn't it seem more vivid, more colorful in other years? Each fall he likes to go somewhere else, to explore new ground, but then it always seems it isn't quite as good a place as last time. And the photographs – they never turn out quite like he thought they would. He must have a thousand pictures of fall colors but only a couple are worth remembering. The camera always makes him nervous. He spends more time looking for the right shot than enjoying the leaves, wondering if he should pull over here or push on around that next hill, worrying that those clouds on the horizon will move in and block the sun. Maybe he shouldn't bring the camera at all, but that would probably make him even more nervous.

So he drives out again, full of anticipation and old worries, but on the trip back home through the darkening hills and smoke from burning grass and leaves, something he can't name stirs in him – a kind of peace, a kind of resolution, or maybe even nostalgia. There's a huge moon rising, a *v* of honking geese, and perhaps later tonight he'll wake up to rain and look out at the falling leaves under the streetlights. It will be a time to sit quietly, perhaps to write something down, a moment when trivial things cease to matter. Autumn after autumn seems to become one in him, and he sits and watches the wet streets filling up with leaves.

A man is driving home with his family from a trip. It is only September but already it's time to turn on the car heater. He watches the dashboard lights – something is wrong with the laboring engine. He worries about stopping way out here in the empty blackness. There are so few cars tonight. Winter will be early again this year. It will cost a lot to get the car running right again, but then there probably won't be any more trips for awhile. When he was in third grade he dropped his jack o'lantern on the front porch steps and it shattered. Perhaps they'll be home in time tonight to watch the late news on TV. If he doesn't watch the red warning light, maybe it won't come on.

Northern lights, the children cry, and around the car are sheets of green and blue, like lightning poured from a bowl. The children press their faces against the side windows; the man drives on, knowing that it might be dangerous to stop the car way out here. He can catch only glimpses of the shimmering fire around them, but he can see the huge orange moon rising in a nest of wispy, low-lying clouds. The car's headlights seem to be flickering. A cup of coffee would taste good now, but it might keep him awake later.

Northern lights, the children cry, and when they finally reach the outskirts of the city the man stops the car beside a plowed field. The lights are almost gone – only a few faint streaks above them. From the north, a chilling wind; even the car seems to be shuddering. The man kicks at dirt clods on the side of the road, and the children dance around to keep warm. Above the city, the moon climbs, distant and white. Hurry up, he tells the children. It's time to go.

A WORKER IN WOOD

AFTER so many years of it, even his face has begun to look like a well-finished piece of wood – smooth and dark and rich, with little intricate whorls around the eyes. He speaks mostly with his hands and shoulders. There isn't much need for words: you can't trust them like you can trust a good piece of oak or cherry. Words are forever splintering or taking on the wrong shades or colors. Words won't fill your pockets or keep the stiffness from your fingers or sharpen a blade.

There's no need to stand around once the bargain is struck. There's too much work to be done, so we leave him, bending low over his workbench, his mouth whispering into the deepest grain.

A RIPE OLD AGE

EVER since he was young he had but one ambition: longevity. Maybe it was the *National Geographic* magazines he'd read as a teenager – all those so-called primitive cultures where everyone lived for such a long time. At least that's the way it looked; after all, like most teenage boys, he never really *read* those magazines. When he was twenty-five, he held a quarter-century party for himself, then marched onward into his fourth and fifth decades. This is wonderful, he thought, just the way he'd planned it. But when he was nearing seventy and his company had retired him, his children chipped in to send him off to a rest home so they could visit him every third or fourth weekend. He lived in a tiny room crowded with artificial flowers and beds and a deaf roommate he couldn't stand. But he lived on, year after year, even when his deaf friend had hanged himself with the cord to his electric razor, even after all his children had died, one by one. Nothing mattered, really, as long as someone renewed his *National Geographic* subscription each year on his birthday. Someday, he knew, the reporters and photographers would come at last, so he sat and waited, well past his first century celebration. And everyone who visited his room on weekends remarked what a coy old philosopher he was, and what a wonderful accomplishment it must be to live to such a ripe old age.

ONE SIZE FITS ALL

THIS is a one cap town, not just in the fields or elevators, but in the restaurants and living rooms as well – Sigco, Treflan, Richland, John Deere, Cat, you name it. Some people worry about their sons using drugs; out here, a mother frets about the day her boy goes off without his cap, but rest assured that few ever do. The streets are full of caps, the bars and shopping mall, even the classrooms. Try to imagine funerals full of dark caps, wedding parties matching tuxedos to caps. The volunteer fire department wears caps under their helmets. The mayor wears a different cap every day. Pity the poor young rebel yearning to be different, who orders his cap from the L. L. Bean catalog or buys one with something cute on it at the county fair. He's likely to come home gobbed to the brim with tobacco juice and lug grease.

Even the females have taken to wearing caps, at least the younger ones. It's getting so it's hard to tell the boys and girls apart, and it's getting hard for some of those youngsters to imagine what it was like before caps. Their grandparents try to tell them about the old days when you had to make your own, but you won't find many who believe a word of it. Not in this town. Not on your bare-headed life.

NIGHT MAN

ALL-NIGHT cafes – you never know where you're going to find them, or who'll be there, except for the ones who think they need to sober up, who can't go home or won't go home, chatting in clusters or sitting alone near edges. Sometimes it all depends on a decent cup of coffee, or watching the bowls of jello cubes revolve in the display case near the door. Then there's the gabby night manager who's just transferred back from the day shift at a cut in pay – because he likes it here, and besides, who can sleep like they used to, anyway? There should be a national register of all-night cafes, he says, a kind of Michelin Guide. He's thought about doing some traveling, you know, and one of those who would come in mighty handy. He glances at his watch: time to get moving. The breakfast crowd starts showing up at six. They're different, you know, make you nervous with all their false starts. You wouldn't want to hang around those people too long. I tried it, he says; I'll try just about anything once, and now I know. You understand, don't you?

RESORT MAN

HE's lived near water fifty years, selling minnows and outboard gas, cleaning other people's fish and listening. All the stories he's heard could fill a bigger lake than this one, he says, sitting in the doorway of the baithouse, watching gulls hover in the wind. But fish? No way. In fifty years he's never wet a line. Why? he says. He'd rather go to St. Louis to see the Cards or just to ride the train. Fifty years in the baithouse, a couple of trips to the Series – a man could do worse, he says, and no, I can't tell you where to find the big ones, but remember Curt Flood? Now there was a rugged piece of work. Took them all to court for trading him after ten seasons. Ruined him, too, he says, fillet knife flashing through another walleye, flipping skin and scales against the wall. Can you imagine? Some people won't ever know why.

THE USED BOOK MAN

ONE bottom shelf is for the books of poems. Even the owner, a man who has traded in books longer than most of us bumping through his cluttered aisles have been reading, has to admit he doesn't know what they're worth. Something, he says. Not as much as they probably should be – not for me, not for those writers. Poets. Most of those books are even signed, but I've been told they'd be worth more if they'd just sign their names, period. But they hardly ever do that. It's always "For Mary, who came to hear me read," or something like that. Most of the time they don't even sign their full names, not even to people they've just met – people who someday are going to sell those books to me for a quarter a pound. "For two new friends, all best, Bill." I've been told that one is famous. What'll you give me for all best, Bill? Not as much as it's worth. I know that.

THE GARBAGE MEN

TEN o'clock. They're always late in nice weather. The city lets them make their own hours – cruising the streets like privateers, scattering birds and traffic, whistling at the bathrobed neighbor who flees from the plastic bags she's just dragged to the curb. Above the big scoop's groan and whine, transistors blare three different stations.

Each week they come back to remind us everything we prize will someday be reduced. Beneath the grime, their bodies gleam – swinging down from the clanging truck, smashing our cans and flattening our lids, grinning at all our secrets.

THE WAY IT GOES

EVERY time they're in the city, Father wants to drive past the house he lived in as a child. That was my room, he tells the family – up there in the back corner, where the elm tree branches used to be. They nod and smile the way they always do. That was where we used to shoot baskets, Father continues, when the garage was still standing. They drive around the block again, and then again, each time noticing something new – the awful color that's been used to paint the trim, the way the house next door has moved a little closer.

The long drive home is silent, Father lost again. Someday, you'll do this too, he tells them. The family dozes in the waning lights of suburbs, sensing the open road at last – farms with yardlights coming on, all those villages scattered through the deepening night.

ROADSIDE ATTRACTION

His name is Moose Dung, a translation from the Indian tongue no one around here speaks. The marker says he was a chief, and so he stands in red and turquoise – fifteen fiberglass feet of him, looking sullenly out across the flat and snowy fields where rivers join beneath the ice. Too far to see that face clearly. But notice this: someday they'll build a model Indian village here to keep him company. Must be a burger stand around here someplace. Drive on.

Daydreamer

BERGY & ME

1. *Blood Brothers*

BERGY and I saw it in the Saturday matinee at the Varsity Theater, so of course we had to try it ourselves. These two guys – a cowboy and an Indian – took knives and cut their wrists and then pressed their two wrists together so they could be "blood brothers." It didn't seem to hurt them. They just acted strong and stared into each other's eyes. It looked real neat.

When we got back home we went out to Bergy's garage to do the ceremony. Bergy got real excited, like I'd never seen him act before. He knew that blood was really blue when it was inside your body, but the instant it touched the air it turned red. He kept looking at the vein on the back of his wrist like this might be the chance to prove something to me.

But our mothers wouldn't let us play with knives, and the old jacknife we found in the vacant lot was so rusty we couldn't even get it open. I did have this safety pin where a button was missing on my shirt, so I thought that might work just as well. After all, it could still draw some blood, couldn't it? That got Bergy mad at me. He said I was a sissy so I pushed him down and sat on his chest till he said I was his best friend, and we finally agreed to try it with the pin. But he got to do the sticking for both of us and we couldn't flinch.

It really hurt, too, but I only jumped a little bit and

Bergy said it was probably okay. But when he saw the blood coming out of the end of my finger he got kind of funny in the face and said that he really had to go home for supper or he'd get a licking for sure. I guess I could have just stood there with blood dripping out of my finger, but I couldn't let Bergy get away with that, so I pushed him down again and took the pin away from him and stuck his finger hard and then pushed our two fingers together so we'd be blood brothers just like in the movie. But Bergy was crying and called me a fat shit and when we were wrestling around on the garage floor he got blood on his shirt and on mine too, and then he went and told his mother and mine about what I had made him do, and I got a licking from my dad who said I'd be lucky if I didn't get an infection in my finger, and Bergy said I'd probably have to go to the doctor and maybe if it got real bad they'd have to cut my finger off or maybe even my whole hand.

Well, I didn't see Bergy for a long time after that because his mother wouldn't let him play with me, and even if I didn't get infected after all, I started wondering what if some of Bergy's blood really got inside of me? It made me real nervous for a long time, like maybe I could feel myself starting to act just like Bergy, and even though we never even talked about being blood brothers again, I had to wonder if Bergy ever got scared that he was starting to act just like me.

2. Lessons

Heave it, Bergy cried. Chuck it, fling it. That's what we did most days – any kind of ball or rock, crabapples, marbles, sticks, whatever we could find in the apartment house garbage out back. Tell me why you boys are always throwing things, my mother said, and I knew the lecture was coming, the one about learning my lesson, the one about putting someone's eye out. I never did, though there were times when I came close – the kid whose glasses I cracked with pebbles in the schoolyard, the daughter of my mother's friend I beaned with a chunk of tar from the street, and even Bergy, the day I laid him out with a softball. Some throw, Bergy said, and didn't come out to play with me for days. Wait till your father gets home, my mother said when she put down the phone. So I waited out in front and bounced a golf ball off the steps and wall until I missed, of course, and broke a basement window. Maybe it was then I learned for the first time about those hopeless laws that bound me. Or maybe it was just the summer afternoon, the thwack of the ball against the bricks, the empty streets and the sidewalks, with not a soul in sight.

3. *Theology*

BERGY said that going to school on Sunday was about the dumbest thing he'd ever heard of – didn't I get enough of school during the week? I tried to show him the presents they gave me, like the picture of Jesus steering the ship. Isn't He supposed to walk on water? Bergy said. What's he need a ship for, anyway? I had to wonder about that one, about the teacher's other stories, too – like all those plagues, or the time God turned the foolish lady into salt. This Sunday stuff was risky business, but Bergy didn't seem to care a bit. His parents didn't even go to church.

There he'd sit on Sunday mornings, out on the front porch with the funny papers, watching me trudge off to Bible class. Ask them to give you some of their wine, he'd yell, and when I finally did, the teacher said I was in big trouble. I prayed to Jesus to get me out of that one, but He never did – sailing off into the clouds with me alone in the corner, and in my foolish mouth the unmistakable taste of salt.

4. *The Silver Screen*

Roy Rogers was King of the Cowboys, Gene Autry the
Prince of the Plains. A king is better than a prince, Bergy
said. Everyone knows you just like Gene Autry because
he's fat, like you. That's the way it went each Saturday,
ten cartoons and a cowboy movie at the Varsity
matinee. The only times we didn't argue were when
they'd bring in Tim Holt or some other commoner. But
there was war, too, and crime fighters. They knew what
would keep us cheering through the Previews, get us
to spend our allowances on Root Beer Barrels and soda
pop – down in the fourth row from the front, where
everything stuck.

And then we'd go home to act out every scene, and
dream ourselves away from tidy houses, parents,
chores. I can't wait to grow up, Bergy said. I wasn't sure
of what he meant by that, except that he was older,
smarter, as he kept reminding me. Maybe he *would* be
King of the Cowboys, galloping off ahead of me each
Saturday – all those winding trails and darkening hills.

5. *Trophies*

THE one time my father took me fishing I caught a little sunfish, which he wanted to put back in the lake. But I had to bring it home to show Bergy, who said it was pretty good, for me. That same day, he and his father had been hiking by the Mississippi and found a big snapping turtle, which was out on Bergy's back porch in a bucket. A bunch of the kids from the neighborhood came over to see it and we all stood around for a long time trying to get it to eat something, trying to get it to snap at sticks. Watch your stupid fingers, Bergy kept saying, waving us back with his mother's yardstick. The next morning I found my sunfish in the garbage, wrapped up in the Sunday comics and beginning to stink.

6. *Sociology*

BERGY said his father was a Chevy man, which meant a Chevy was the only kind of car he'd ever own. When I asked my father about that, he said he'd owned a Chevy once, too, but then a Dodge and two Fords because those were what he'd gotten the best deals on. What was I do to about that kind kind of indifference, anyway? Without an argument, Bergy decided we were Ford people, pure and simple. At least we were second best.

Let's talk about Republicans and Democrats, Bergy said, but I couldn't bear the thought of what I'd probably find out — even if I didn't know what those words meant. At least we weren't Nash people or Studebaker people. Bergy decided it wasn't so bad being Ford people as long as there was *somebody* to make fun of. I had to admit my relief. I had to hand it to him for *that*.

7. Killing Time

It was on the bridge over the railroad tracks where we'd walk sometimes on our way to look for empty Coke bottles by the university – where, if we lucky, we could stand in the flood of smoke and steam from those old engines chuffing underneath us. Just like the fog in monster movies, Bergy would say. Leave it to Bergy to come up with a good adventure for free, even if we'd have to wait for hours to find it.

But there'd also be our mothers wringing hands over all those little burn holes in our clothes, the reek of smoke that stayed with us. Sometimes in bed at night I could smell it, and I'd remember Bergy's face disappearing for a moment in that fog, the engine moving off down the tracks, the blurry, stinging eyes, and then the caboose – a point of reflected light in the distance, fading fast.

8. Hopeless Case

In our apartment house, Bergy had the corner on emptying trash for all the old ladies. Each day I'd watch him hauling bags out back to the garbage cans and incinerator, and then on Saturday morning he'd collect his money – right before we'd head off to the matinee at the Varsity. Buck seventy-five this week, he'd say, rubbing his hands together. That's not counting tips. Tips of *what?* I'd say, and Bergy would roll his eyes.

Once when I was sick or maybe just too lazy, my mother even paid Bergy to empty *our* trash. That meant no movies on Saturday for me, no candy either. Sorry to do this to you, Bergy said, but business is business. Who was I to argue? Bergy had a bank account. He had a paper route, too, ran errands up and down the block, stole all the empty pop bottles off the back porches before I even knew they were there. I was probably home waiting for our wastebaskets to fill up, hoping one of my teeth might somehow fall out – anything would do, as long as I had money for Saturday, and maybe even enough left over to buy a couple of Bergy's old comic books.

Spend it all again this week? Bergy would say, which is just what my father said. What did they know, anyway? *All* of them who frowned at me, jingling their stupid pockets – jingling, jingling, jingling as they walked away.

GOOD teeth run in my family, Bergy told me. He'd never had a filling at the dentist's office, even if he ate just as much candy as I did. He'd laugh when I tried to tell him about that terrifying drill. He really laughed when I told him about the time the lady at the dentist's office popped out three of my rotten baby teeth when she was flossing me.

You didn't even bring them home with you? Bergy said. That's twenty-five cents apiece you blew. I couldn't figure his arithmetic – *my* tooth fairy only paid a dime. Tooth fairy? Bergy said. You know your old man is the tooth fairy, don't you? And then he started in on Santa Claus and the Easter Bunny.

It was hard to figure, all that stuff Bergy told me – at least he didn't ruin Halloween. My bellyache did that, after we'd eaten all our candy in one sitting, as my mother said. Actually, we were standing out behind the garages when I started to feel it, drunk with candy – all my teeth going rotten at once. But this time I was going to pull them out myself, long before that dentist's lady ever got hold of me. And then I was going to have a talk with my father about the going rate for teeth under my pillow.

Sure you will, Bergy said, flashing me another of his perfect grins.

10. *Entrepreneur*

BERGY decided we had to have a Kool-aid stand – if I'd get my mother to make the Kool-aid, that is; if I could get her to loan us the card table, and buy some paper cups. He'd take care of the money. He'd even make a sign if I could find some old paint in the garage – oh, and a brush, too, and a big piece of cardboard. He'd see if he could swipe some masking tape.

There we sat on the corner the two hottest, muggiest days of August – dog days, my mother called them, though we didn't see any dogs and not many people either. Just a couple of nuns from the little convent a block away. Bergy called them penguins, but not me. I didn't dare to. And I didn't dare to tell him how much they scared me or how sometimes they'd show up in my bad dreams. Most of the time, it seemed, those nuns were watching us from across the street.

Oh, a car stopped once to ask directions, and our fathers each bought a glass or two when they came home from work, but mostly all we had to show for our efforts were the red rings around our mouths. Get your cherry beer, five cents a glass, Bergy would shout to the nuns, and then he'd disappear for awhile – he had to help his mother with the wash, he said, or run an errand for his aunt.

I never told Bergy that one time when he left, two of those old penguins finally crossed the street and bought two glasses of Kool-aid without even speaking to me, or how my hand shook when I reached out for that warm, damp dime the tall one fished out from somewhere in all that black she wore. I never told him either how I dreamed that I was going straight to hell, or how I kept that dime hidden in my pocket, for weeks – where I could feel it from time to time, slowly burning that hole I'd been warned about.

11. *Sex Education*

We saw them floating in the gutter on a rainy day –
three balloons, I thought, but Bergy said not to pick
them up. You don't know anything, he said. Those are
rubbers, what men put on their wienies. You want to
touch something like that? Bergy knew everything
when it came to men and women, knew about morfa-
dikes and why they kept those jars of dead babies in
the zoology lab at the university, the place we'd
sometimes sneak into on Saturdays. What he didn't
know was about my grandfather's medical book my
cousin and I had discovered one day during summer
vacation. The skin diseases were the worst, the woman
with a baby coming out of her a close second.

We never found a morfadike in the book – I did tell
Bergy that – and rubbers weren't there either. Who's
your friend, Bergy said, me or that stupid book? I had
to wonder where Bergy got his information, though
he *was* older, had his own room and comic books my
mother didn't even want me to know about. One thing's
for certain when it came to Bergy: I never knew what
dark, goose-bumpy thing he'd tell me next. And some-
day, I was hoping, he'd have to get to the most impor-
tant things. He'd have to tell me why.

12. *Slow Learner*

IT's time you learned how to smoke, Bergy said. His old man puffed on a pipe so it was up to me to swipe a cigarette from mine. What if he counts them? I asked. Don't be a girl, Bergy said, which is the one thing I didn't want to be. So, late that night when I couldn't sleep I took a Raleigh cork-tip from the pack on the kitchen table. I like Luckies better, Bergy said, but I suppose this will do the trick. What trick was that? The way I coughed and rubbed my burning eyes, or the way I threw up on the basement steps? And how had Bergy ever gotten me to that dark old basement where we both knew there were rats? Our mothers had seen them down there when they washed clothes.

Just like I thought, Bergy said – you're a girl. And then he told everyone at school the way my face turned green. It was the rats, I lied. I saw a rat when we were down there – even Bergy was afraid to mess with rats. That's when he started calling me Rat Boy. I couldn't even tell my mother, knowing I'd get a licking if she found out I was down the basement with Bergy. Well, maybe it wasn't so bad being Rat Boy, I kept telling myself. At least I wasn't a girl.

13. *Saving Up*

MORE than anything, I wanted a new fielder's glove, but my mother said we'd have to wait until we had enough Raleigh coupons. Half our apartment, it seemed, was from coupons or stamps – S&H Green Stamps or Gold Bond Stamps and some others I can't even remember, only that sometimes I'd sit there and finger those fat books of stamps and piles of coupons held together with rubber bands, imagining they were real money and what I was going to buy with them. There wasn't much in those catalogs that interested me – dishes, toasters, floorlamps, stuff for my baby sister. Besides, we had most of it already.

The Raleigh catalog did have a fielder's glove, and even if it wasn't quite what I had in mind I knew it was the only one I had a chance of getting. Right after we get the last chair for the card table, my father told me. That's what he'd been saving up for, so that had to come first.

I asked all my friends if their fathers smoked Raleigh cigarettes but none of them did, though Bergy told me he was getting a catcher's mitt for his birthday and his father didn't even smoke cigarettes.

I'd just have to be patient, my mother said. Besides, it wouldn't be baseball season for another couple of months. I knew my father couldn't smoke enough in that short time to get all the coupons we'd need for that fielder's glove. It'd be Halloween if I was lucky, but that was when I was hoping for a new football.

You can't get something for nothing, my mother said. I tried to remember that each time I saw her licking stamps when she got home from the grocery store, each time I saw my father lighting up a cigarette. How old did I have to be, anyway, before I got as smart as they were?

14. *Crime & Punishment*

EVERYBODY knew it wasn't very hard to swipe something from the little five and dime in our neighborhood. Some of the boys in my room at school used to make a game of it – plastic cars, baseball cards, comic books. The only kid I ever saw get caught was swiping comic books. I used to dream about the man who ran the store dragging him off to some back room. That kid just looked at me standing in the aisle with my hands in my pockets, as if to say he knew that I was guilty too. I had to be.

Well, I wasn't – not then anyway. Bergy said that kid would probably go to prison but it wouldn't be as bad as what his parents did to him. Maybe if I took something for my sister it wouldn't count. Any little thing would do, just to show the boys at school. It wasn't enough anymore to take the nickels I'd find around the apartment for candy and gum. I had to take that little doll, inside my stocking cap. Nothing to it, I bragged to my school friends – who were expecting something more. The hard part was putting it back the next day, just after the dime store man stopped me to ask how my father was doing. How did he know my father, anyway? And who else did he know?

Bergy didn't believe me when I told him. No one did. But it didn't matter. I knew I wouldn't be swiping anything else from that five and dime. I knew too that my mother probably left those nickels out on purpose.

I could see it in the grown-ups, all of them – everything I thought I understood and didn't. Everything I thought I'd hidden – written all over my guilty little face.

15. *Bazooms*

WHAT'S the strongest thing in the world? Bergy asked. A bra, he said, falling down on the grass. Because it holds up two milk factories. That was the funniest joke I'd ever heard, at twelve anyway. Bazooms, Bergy said, waving his fingers in circles and rolling his eyes. Bazooms, like in his *National Geographics*, but it sure was hard to believe that the girls in our class would ever grow up like that, except for maybe Shari across the street who was a year older and some of the ninth and tenth graders were starting to come over and give her rides on their bikes. Shari had real bazooms, like those ladies we'd watch in the grocery store every day, bending for stuff on the lower shelves. Ain't summer great, Bergy said, and each night we'd walk my dog around every block in the neighborhood, looking for bazooms in windows. We never did see any, but my father said how nice it was to see me take some responsibility for a change, that maybe I was learning something after all and he sure hoped it wasn't going to change. Not a chance, Bergy said, and rolled his eyes at me, but all I was thinking about was Shari's dark window and all those stupid bikes in her front yard.

HOW I FLUNKED KNOT-TYING

It was in Mrs. K's kindergarten at Marcy School, about the second week of class, and who could have believed that kindly grandmother of a lady would suddenly decide that her pupils should at least know how to tie a simple knot. "It isn't very hard at all," she said, passing out thick green school pencils to us all, along with pieces of string about a foot in length. "Watch carefully now," she told us, demonstrating the proper technique, and before long most of her pupils had it down pat. Except for me, because I was so fascinated by the new green pencil that I hadn't listened to her instructions, which probably wasn't the first time that had happened. Maybe it had been a bad day for her, or maybe I just deserved it. What she needed was to make a good example for all of her pupils by holding up my new green pencil just beyond my grasp, and my limp, knotless string. "This will never do," she clucked and her jowls flapped and my knees knocked, and everybody was gathered around us laughing, and this one kid who probably went to Sunday school in a three-piece suit even then suddenly handed Mrs. K *his* pencil with a perfect two inch row of knots topped off by a bow – the kind my mother tied my shoes with, the kind that was still a complete mystery to most of us. He just handed it to Mrs. K with a flourish, and didn't say anything at all.

The next day, which was Saturday, I spent the

entire morning by the radio, tying knots – rows of them, yards of them, on every pencil I could find. Someday, someday they would tear that old school down and I would be there to watch, wearing beautiful bows.

THE WEIRD KID

CHARLIE was the weird kid – there's always one in every class, and even if I've forgotten his last name, I haven't forgotten that it was in fifth grade with a teacher none of us liked very much. And I still remember him every time I see a ball-point smudge, for Charlie was one long streak of smeared ink. He seemed to ooze ink, and cowlicks, and ripped seams, and tardy slips. He was the suicidal one who perfected the head-first slide in baseball – on a gravel playground. He was the kid whose homework was never done, who always smelled funny and had fuzzy teeth, who tracked in mud from the school yard and got sent back to clean his shoes three or four times till he got it right.

Charlie was the only kid I ever knew who dared to let farts during the flag salute. He was the only kid who was crazy enough to dip Mary Kay's braids in an ink bottle; she was the one beautiful girl in the fifth grade, and Charlie must have known that five or six of the hulking types would be waiting for him after school to pulverize him for Mary Kay's honor and their pleasure. And it was Charlie who told me my first really filthy joke – in fact, he told the whole class, one day when the teacher decided to indulge us all with a new kind of fun called "Joke Sharing Hour," which, thanks to Charlie, lasted only about five minutes and was never held again, not even on the best of days.

And long after all the beautiful Mary Kays were married off and manufacturing beautiful children, long after the Wallys and Steves had packed away their baseball gear forever, long after the Geralds and Dianas had won full scholarships to the graduate schools of their choice, Charlie is the one I still wonder about. He's probably a bartender or a race car driver or a deck hand – whatever it is, he's not very good at it, still sweating out a lifetime of principals' offices. But I wish I had him here right now – maybe to thank him, to tell him that even if all of us were embarrassed about him and really didn't like him very much, he was a kind of martyr we could always count on to take the heat off everyone else. I'd at least like to show him what I've written about him, to show him the way I still smudge my own ink, and tell him that sometimes now I'm even able to admit it.

WHAT I REMEMBER ABOUT THE SIXTH GRADE

OUR room lost the school softball championship when that four-eyed kid popped out with the bases loaded. We did win the spelling bee, though. Weird Charlie said it was because we had the ugliest girls.

The Scarlet Tanager edged out the Wood Duck in our balloting for the State Bird because the girls got organized when they found out the teacher liked red. I voted for the Bluejay, or maybe it was the Loon. Weird Charlie voted for the Crow.

The teacher nearly got knocked out cold when a big portrait of George Washington or somebody famous fell off the wall and conked her on the head. Most of the girls cried. Most of the boys laughed, especially Weird Charlie.

Once a month or so they'd herd us to the school basement for atomic bomb drills and films of houses exploding in firestorms. When it came to the Nuclear Age, even Weird Charlie learned to keep his mouth shut.

FAMILY SECRET

SOME of us never survived the Depression, my grand-mother used to tell me. I never knew what that meant until the time my father tried to stretch a tank of gas because it was a few cents cheaper in St. Cloud. When we ran out, it was two miles from town and right next to the state reformatory. I can still see my father trudging off along the road, head down, while my mother and I watched the walls, the guard turrets watching us. I was sure there'd be a break any minute, sure those desperate convicts would come to get us. I'd seen those prison movies, after all, and we were going to die. My only bright thought was that somehow it would serve my father right.

And so we watched, counting bricks until my father came back with a can of cheap St. Cloud gas. All my mother said was try to understand – he's had to pay a lot more than he bargained on. But what did I know about paying, anyway? What did I know about saving pennies or surviving? And what in the world would I ever know about desperate men?

SAM HILL, JACK ROBINSON, AND ME

"Where in the Sam Hill have you been?" my father yells at me. I don't know who this Sam Hill is, but he always makes my father angry. I just hate it when Sam Hill's around with his beady little face, always waiting to make trouble when my father gets home. And that's not to mention his friend Jack Robinson. My father says he's going to paddle my buttix as quick as Jack Robinson – who's the one who teaches fathers how to paddle. It's getting so this place isn't big enough for the three of us any more. A couple of us are going to have to go – and some days now, I get the feeling that one of them is going to be me.

THE FAT KID

WHEN my waist size loomed larger than my father's, he got concerned. "Baby fat" was what I'd heard for years. What I'd heard from the old woman who lived downstairs and brought me milk and plates of cookies was, "Will you mother let you eat this? You'd better go upstairs and check." "The kid's a lummox," said my father, who had a different way with words.

I used to dream they'd invent a blubber machine to strip away the fat, or that someday I'd find a loose thread in my belly, and when I tugged it all those pounds would unravel like a bulky sweater. Fat kids believe in science and magic, in mothers who love them, in second helpings that don't count if nobody sees them, in fathers who are mostly gone on trips.

Lardass, blimp, and fatty, fatty two-by-four, I heard them all. Each school I went to had more skinny kids — how did they do it, anyway? Someday I'd know. Someday I'd find the secret thread. Someday I'd go back and tell that grinning old woman what she could do with her cookies. Someday, when they didn't taste so good.

THE MAN WHO HOLDS THE CAMERA

In the photograph, I'm the one who keeps his head down, showing teeth. It's hard to smile when you're squinting into sun. It's hard to look excited after riding for hours in the back seat, watching the tops of trees. But this is the country and we're having fun. Smile, my father says in double-breasted gabardine and felt hat shadowing his eyes – the hat I play with when he's not looking, when I drive my pot-lid car in the kitchen, to New York or to India, never to the country in the flat, still light of Sunday afternoon. Smile for the camera, my father says – he's not in many pictures, I noticed even then.

The faces pale, my mother's red dress slips to rusty brown, all else to shades of gray. We're in the country, having fun on Sunday afternoon – squinting at the man who holds the camera, trying hard to smile.

ATTENTION SPAN

My grandfather was the only grownup who never asked me what I'd be when I grew up. When everybody else made plans, he'd slip me money for the movies, or take me riding in his big green car. Sometimes he'd sing or tell a story, but mostly we didn't talk, because we didn't have to. What really mattered was the way he fixed things – fevers, cuts, all kinds of aches.

And now I remember my father in restaurants, sitting at the head of the table with grandchildren on either side, making sure each waitress knew that they were his. And then he'd hand me a wet-diapered baby. Here, he'd say, this is your job, I've had my turn.

Sometimes it seems I've spent my life watching old men. Just when I least expect it, they creep into my dreams with blankets. How old are your kids getting, anyway? they whisper. You never were one to pay attention, were you. Tell us again what you think you've learned.

NOTHING

You've spent your money, now what do you have to show for it? was what my father always asked – the man who never bought anything, who invested in it. Nothing, I'd say. Nothing. And he'd just shake his head. Maybe next time I'd invest in something, though I wasn't sure what it could be – this notebook, maybe, each page filled up, then torn out. Nothing, all over again. Or maybe the ballgame I went to yesterday, a two hitter, and when I got home I just wanted to call my father and tell him all about it, except of course he was dead, and now I'm down to the last notebook page. What do you have to show for it? Nothing, I say. Just me. Just you. I didn't even get the cheap seats like you taught me, and I'm glad. That's the way it should be, and it's taken me all this time to say it. Nothing. Nothing. Nothing. And I'm glad.

INSOMNIAC

MAYBE it was the JESUS ON BOARD sign in the window of the blue Omega on the interstate, or maybe the humidity covering the bed like mosquito netting. Whatever the reason, we've been here before – the cricket in the wall and I, this motel, any motel, throbbing our own dark music.

Somewhere a kitchen bulb still burns – my father at the table eating bread and warm milk in his underwear, thumbing his *Reader's Digest.* You'd better have some, he says, not looking up, not asking why I didn't make the team or what I haven't finished. No, we'll just sit here awhile together, sweating, listening to a cricket in the wall, while Jesus drives the backroads, searching for first light.

DAYDREAMER

I AM twelve years old, helping my father with storm windows. Since I am afraid to climb the long, shaky ladder, and not strong enough to slide the heavy windows up to him, my job is to wash them with soapy water from a bucket, spray them with the hose and wipe them down – but there are always streaks, no matter how careful I am, no matter how much time I take. It's too hot to be putting up storm windows, but we have to do it because my father is going to be gone and already yellow leaves are dropping from the elms. Storm windows are leaning against the side of the house, against the apple tree, against the porch steps. Do them over if you can't get the streaks out, my father says, taking off his sweat-soaked shirt. I know I'll never have muscles like his. I know too I'll never be able to climb that ladder – not the way he does, like the trapeze man I saw at the circus once. Hurry up, says the voice from the top of the ladder. Haven't you noticed how late it's getting? And all around us there are snowflakes, white curtains of snowflakes, gliding and shifting with every breath we take.

Talismans

LETTERS FROM OLD FRIENDS

SOMETIMES they arrive like suitors with tattered flowers, polite and threadbare, almost afraid to speak. The weather has been good, hasn't it; there is much to be done. After awhile they get up to leave, thankful to be through with it, backing toward the door and bowing with many kind wishes. Perhaps they will be back, but not for a long time.

Sometimes they arrive like messengers with trumpets, elegant in their tight gold suits, a little flash of something not quite seen, a promise that the emissary will arrive one day – soon, they insist, very soon.

Sometimes they are like tired old widows in black, stocky duennas whose faces are hidden by their shadowy veils. They sit in the most uncomfortable chairs, wringing their hands, their tiny jade rosaries. Then, just when you think they will disappear completely, they move closer, stretching out to pat your arm. You settle back in your chair and the fireplace warms your face, filling all the damp spaces with waves of yellow light.

CLOTHESLINES

Most of them are abandoned now in the backyards –
only here and there a beach towel hangs, or a bathing
suit, a pair of sneakers or a chamois cloth. No mothers
running out just before the rain. No glum children wip-
ing down the lines with rags, or hanging on them –
like I did. I even broke one once, trying to make some
kind of giant slingshot.

On wash days, my mother lugged the wicker basket
up the steps from the basement laundry room, the
smell of blueing rising from her dress. "Good drying
weather," she'd say, and I'd hand her the clothespins
one by one, the little stiff-legged creatures who some-
times were my toys on days it rained – or the other kind,
with springs, we'd make into shooters for stolen wooden
matches. "What's been happening to all my clothes-
pins?" my mother would ask, and then she'd hang out
the rugs and beat them. It should have been me – beater
or beaten, hanger on clotheslines, stealer of pins. It
should have been, but it never was, and my mother
brought in loaded baskets that smelled of sun and trees.
Sometimes I'd help her sprinkle clothes before she
ironed – or souse my sister with the bottle, or chase
my sister's grass-stained knees between the sheets that
flapped like flags and banners – out in the backyard,
where mothers watched their children dance between
the soaring sails.

BLACK COFFEE

I LEARNED how to drink coffee in college – the first time I had to stay up all night to study for an exam. That's what makes you a real college student, my friends said, even if you have to load it up with milk and sugar. I couldn't stop thinking about my parents. Coffee is what parents drink.

When I went home for Christmas vacation, I asked my parents for a cup of coffee, probably hoping it would shock everybody, but my father just kidded me about adding all that milk and sugar. If you're going to drink coffee, he said, learn to drink it the right way – black.

So, that's how we do it. Even when I visited in the East and drank their bitter mud, I didn't put anything in it. You must be from the Midwest, one waitress said – nobody else is nuts enough to drink it black.

Nobody else. My grandmother stirring raw eggs into ground coffee to brew it in the Norwegian way, boiled in a big enamel pot, clear and ever-flowing. Catch the bubbles in your spoon before they hit the rim, my mother said, and you'll come into money. I sure could go for another cup, my father said – secure in his faith that in his house everyone drank their coffee black and the pot was always on.

FIREWORKS

A WEEK before the Fourth and they're popping all over the neighborhood – the little ones are all that are legal now, the ones we used to call ladyfingers, the ones we wouldn't be caught dead with.

You'll put an eye out, my grandmother said every day. She was certain of it. I hated to disappoint her, but that's what I did best – blowing her jar lids thirty feet in the air, blowing up my model planes, vegetables from the garden, dolls and toy cars, grasshoppers and garter snakes. Your cousin lost his finger, Grandma said, but I knew that was from a blasting cap, not a firecracker. My cousin told me he couldn't figure out what it was so he thought he'd take it apart and then it went off and he was sitting there staring at the place his finger used to be.

I used to dream about missing eyes or fingers, that legion of wounded boys who didn't listen to their grandmothers. Even now, I have that dream sometimes – there must be a lot of us who do. Tell me, Grandma says, what are you going to do when you've spent all your money on fireworks? What are you going to do when you've blown everything up?

GRACKLES

"GET out of here!" My grandmother cruised her backyard chasing black shadows with a broom. "Pesky things!" she screeched, "just like some kids can be," and I too fled her gardener's stare.

All summer it was a battle to save her berries from those raucous, ugly birds. She put up scarecrows, pinwheels, everything that never worked, and there she stood in her garden, straw hat akimbo, arms flailing like a North Dakota windmill, while small boys hid in bushes, waiting for the all-clear.

Grackles. They gather now in my own backyard, as if they're waiting for me to come outside. "Go away, you pesky things," I say from the window, just as I was taught. But my heart isn't in it. No berries here to defend, no grandmothers, and no little boys.

FIRST SNOW

IT gets dark by five o'clock now, as I watch bare branches quivering outside my office window. It has been such a long day in its shortness, and now I'll close the door and hope no one knows I'm still here, hoarding the last half-hour for myself. It's so hard to get up from this chair and struggle with winter clothes, my head full of wind chill warnings – and even on my fifteen minute walk home, even in my new coat, I know the cold will shake me.

By the time I get outside, the wind has dropped away and it's snowing hard – the first snow of winter, sifting through the branches, muffling my footsteps on the sidewalk. In each house there is a light in the front windows, hazy through a curtain of snow, covering porch steps and roofs and all the unraked leaves. Snow falling into muddy river water, fields of sunflowers with their heads down, deserted country roads. Snow falling inward, through the body, settling between bones, heavy with winter sleep.

NAPS

First, you need a sofa, Saturday afternoon with sports on TV – golf is best, or baseball, something slow and deliberate, but it doesn't really matter. The family tip-toes by, grinning. You really should be outside, you know – not many nice days left. You remember kinder-garten, lying on your blanket, staring up at Teacher's massive legs, your mother calling you in from play – why was it you never could sleep then?

Outside, the BigWheels cruise the neighborhood. Not many nice days left. The sofa bobs on lake waves, veers and dips on humming tires, and somewhere, far, far away a ball is soaring into brilliant sun. It never comes down.

HERON

Surprised by the boat, the great blue heron screeches, lifts off from his station in the tall reeds, his slow wings scooping sultry air above our heads, then disappearing into mist on the far shore. The fishing has been dismal all month, too many storms and tricky winds, yet still we come to lose our tackle in the weeds. Two more hours without a good strike, the trolling motor's acting up again, what is it that we're doing wrong? If we talked we'd just make excuses, so we don't talk.

And then the heron passes over, glides, and lifts deliberately, above the trees. I can't help but think of birds from poems – Hughes's crow, Stevens's blackbird, Shelley's skylark. But this is no blithe spirit – a bird that was, that is, that will be back. And so will we, waiting by reeds. His reeds.

SLEEPING TILL NOON

UPSTAIRS, my daughter lies swaddled in her bedsheets like an Eastern princess. Good sleeping weather last night – any summer night is good for her. Lawnmowers, barking dogs, phone calls, the man next door scraping paint to raucous music – none of it matters to her, and I won't wake her either, not for anything less than the Second Coming. Not till noon, anyway. That's when my father's voice takes over. I can't help it. When I grew up, certain things were always held sacred – long distance calls, cleaning your plate, getting up at a "decent" hour.

But let's face it – I don't sleep so well anymore, no matter what my intentions. Sunlight shakes me like there's something urgent I've forgotten. Alarm clocks follow me into every room.

So sleep well, daughter, sleep well for both of us on this fine summer morning. I'll take the phone off the hook, go outside and speak to birds and garbage trucks, and when we meet on the stairs it will be with guilty smiles. Here's one thing, at least, I haven't managed to forget. Good morning, daughter. And yes, indeed, it was.

THE BARBERSHOP

I'VE been coming here for years, one of those places that never changes – not the sounds and smells, not the ten-pound walleye mounted on the wall, not the teenage boys thumbing *Playboy* in the corner. All talk is familiar, brief – the price of gas, the weather, the fishing trips we didn't take. Just as I'm ready to leave, to feel again the the chilly wind across my neck, a mother brings her small son to the chair. He rolls his head and giggles, reaches out to touch the pile of clipped hair on the floor. The barber scoops him up and asks a dozen questions while the small boy grins and rolls his eyes, his beautiful blank eyes. He cannot answer, reaching out, amazed, to touch the barber's face.

I leave them there and for a moment everything freezes – the mother smiling fiercely by the chair, the barber lost in his slow and gentle work, bending now to whisper something secret in that tiny ear.

A CORNER ROOM NEAR THE STAIRS

Iт's impossible to imagine all who've stayed here before
me, what they've added or taken away – how they've
clung to each other or shouted, how they've laughed
or paced the night alone, how they've sat by the win-
dow and watched the lights coming on all the way to
the river. Down the hall, the elevator bell sounds the
hour, and in the lamplight from the writing desk
everything looks all right. What more for this moment
could one ask? Not to be famous or grand, just to be
here – quiet, worn, deliberate – trying to imagine who
has stayed here in this place before me. One of those
necessary stops along the way.

ALL STARS

Tonight the All-Star game is on TV – we watch it every year, those of us who played on teams, in sandlots, alleys, between parked cars. The fat kids who couldn't slide, who batted left and last, got beaned, got banished to right field since no one ever hit it there. The odd kids who dreamed through summer afternoons alone, the kings of r.b.i. – if baseballs were crabapples and bats were sawed-off brooms.

Tonight we're sleek and nonchalant in our fine blue uniforms, shagging long fly balls with one hand, batting cleanup, listening to the crowd go wild at the sweet shock of our lumber meeting waist-high fastballs. And then we'll lope around the base paths waving caps and arms – through the final turn we've been waiting for, heading for home at last.

BLUES IN B-FLAT

How was I to know my roommates wouldn't let me keep that trumpet? It sounded like such a good idea, and only twenty-five bucks from this guy I met in a bar. We'd each had a few beers and when we got to talking he brought the case out from under the table. The horn was an old timer, a little dented but not too bad, just like the one I had in junior high. He played a couple riffs and we talked some more – he could have been good, you know, if he'd kept with it, but school got in the way, and his job, and now he needed twenty-five bucks for a bus ticket to get back home. Wouldn't it be a kick for me to play again? I was pretty good once, wasn't I?

I'd forgotten how long it takes to get your lip back in shape. I'd forgotten the four of us in that little house, with midterms coming up. Every place I tried to practice was the wrong place. It got so bad I had to sit in my closet with the door closed and an old sock stuffed in the bell of the horn. But even that wasn't enough for my roommates. How foolish and inconsiderate could I be, anyway, not to mention my crimes against music?

So I took the trumpet back to the bar one night and waited until this guy came over and asked me what I had in the case. It turns out he'd been a trumpet player, too, once upon a time – couldn't stop fingering those valves. I could see in his eyes I had him. Twenty-five bucks was the easy part. I should have gotten more. I should have known better, too. A few nights later when I happened to go back to the bar, there he was in the corner booth talking to this other guy, with the trumpet on the table between them. I left before he saw me and I never went back to that place again.

When I was a kid, my parents tried to talk me into playing something practical like the piano, but of course I didn't pay any attention. There was something about that shiny trumpet that wouldn't let go of me – something secret, something grand. Even now I have to wonder what would've happened if I'd stayed with it the first time, even the second time. I have to wonder too about that twenty-five dollar trumpet in the bar. It wouldn't surprise me one bit to find out it's still making the circuit, week by week. After all, there are still a lot of us around.

ITALIAN BRIAR

YESTERDAY I bought a new pipe, the first one in over a year, and as I sit in the kitchen trying to teach it to fit my mouth there is early morning sunlight dappling my legs. Last night was so cool and lovely that I slept better than I have in this whole month of July, in spite of the dream about the elevator, and this weekend there will be fishing, and I am really happy for this moment, which surprises me. New pipes and fishing and cool nights in mid-summer aren't enough to base your life on – I know that. Maybe I should go to the office and try to get caught up for a change. Maybe I should weed the garden or fix the back door, like I promised. Or maybe I should turn up that old blues tune on the radio. I know I've heard it before, somewhere, as sunlight falls on the dark knobby wood in my hand, the smoke drifting through the window screens toward all the children coming out to play.

SUMMER SAUSAGE

My father has brought it home again, wrapped in heavy butcher paper from some strange little town in Wisconsin. He's scouted for years to find the right place to buy summer sausage – one of the few good things about being on the road so much, he says. But why do they call it summer sausage? I need to know that, deep in the snow of January. It's taken me an hour just to shovel a path from the back door to the garage, and last week I froze my ears on the way to school. Summer sausage, dark and spicy. It still doesn't make sense, but I know I'll be tasting it for a long time, hearing the knife click against the kitchen table – where my father slices summer sausage, lost in swirling snow.

MIXED FRUIT

In the nursing home, my grandmother was known as a hoarder. Every time we'd visit she'd have a bag full of those little packets of jelly to send home with us. The children thought it was pretty neat – until we'd discover that nine out of ten of those packets were Mixed Fruit, which nobody liked, especially the children. For a long time after the grape and strawberry were eaten up, the raspberry and orange marmalade, there were coffee cans full of Mixed Fruit packets in the cupboard. We couldn't bear to throw them away, knowing how hard Grandma had worked to save them, clearing them into her pockets after everyone else had left the table. A lot of these old people don't care much for packaged jelly, she told me. They're too used to home made.

I didn't think about it until years after my grandmother was dead, but those jelly packets were all she had to give us. And now, every so often in a restaurant when the waitress brings Mixed Fruit, I still can't bear to see it thrown away. I always leave that jelly packet where someone might see it and put it in a pocket. You never know when you'll need to have something to save, something to give away.

LATE NIGHT CALLS

Sometimes when the phone rings late at night I think of my friend Jim. "Did I wake you?" he'd say, and even if he did, I'd never tell him. "Read me something you've written," he'd say. "I need to hear what you've been doing." So I'd read to him and he'd say, "Jesus, that's lovely," or "read it again, brother, this time slower – something's not quite right in those first few lines." And then, of course, he'd read to me – about the farm in Indiana or the old queens at the steam baths where he went sometimes or the Yei-bet-chi dancers he saw once on the way back to Gallup. How different we are, he'd joke, and then I'd try to joke about how late night phone calls usually mean bad news. And Jim would say, "You know I'm bad news, always have been," and we'd talk about what ailed us or writing in bus stations and all-night cafes, or when I was going to come down and see him.

There aren't many people you can call when you're not sleeping, you know. I've been waiting these last few years for someone else to phone late at night, to read poems or ask me to read what I've been working on – just because it needs to be heard. "Jesus," Jim would say, "this dying is hard work, isn't it."

FISHING WITH MY FATHER

I CAN'T remember going fishing as a child more than a few times, mostly with my father. I didn't understand until years later that he really didn't like to fish – once when I tried to explain to him my need to trail hooks in the water down where you can't see anything, wondering what's there and not there and sometimes not even caring, daydreaming of the great pike circling and bass plunging in the reeds. "You catch them," he said, "and I'll help you eat them." So I throw the bait out again and one of these times the rod will jump and bend and I'll set the hook, feeling the old thrill rise through me, taut and quick. "You never know what you'll bring back, do you?" my father said. Yes, tomorrow, if this weather holds, I'll be going fishing, and tonight there is only the restless and fleeting sleep.

MISSING YOU

THE clock radio is on again, and I can't remember set-ting it. This time it's country-western – another sad song about empty arms and empty dreams, empty pickup trucks and empty jukeboxes. Lord, will it ever end? Right now the grandfather clock downstairs would be chiming three or four A.M. if I had remembered to wind it, and if I roll over in bed I'll find that you aren't there, so I just won't roll over. Another cliché drops on my head. Sometimes it's hard to keep from cryin', the radio says, and I've limped down the hallway of another blank page. I know you'll be home in a few days, but if this doesn't stop pretty soon I'm going to find myself really listening to that station, and if this don't stop before long I'm goin' out and get me a big steel guitar.

SMALL CRAFT WARNINGS

This is the time when I'm alone in the kitchen early Saturday or Sunday morning. There has been a light snow in the night and I look out to bird and rabbit tracks in the yard. Then, the cheerful Scandinavian voice on the radio reminds me the wind chill is plunging this morning and not to go outside unless I have to.

Well, I don't have to. The paper girl has made it through the dark with her sled and moon boots. I pace the downstairs making promises to empty rooms, checking the furnace gauges, waiting for the house to set sail in the rising wind. Coffee steams on the stove. Eight bells. Everyone I love is asleep.

MARK Vinz was born in North Dakota, grew up in Minneapolis and the Kansas City area, attended the Universities of Kansas (B.A. and M.A. in English) and New Mexico (Ph.D.), and since 1968 has taught at Moorhead State University, where he is presently Professor of English. His poems and stories have appeared in approximately 150 periodicals and anthologies, such as *Poetry Northwest, North American Review, Minnesota Monthly, North Dakota Quarterly, Georgia Review, South Dakota Review, College English, Antioch Review, The Quarterly, Heartland II: Poets of the Midwest* (Northern Illinois University Press), *Poetspeak* (Bradbury Books), and *A Geography of Poets* (Bantam Books). Vinz is also the author of several collections of poetry including *The Weird Kid* (New Rivers Press, 1983), *Climbing the Stairs* (Spoon River Poetry Press, 1983), *Mixed Blessings* (Spoon River Poetry Press, 1989), and *Minnesota Gothic,* to be published by Milkweed Editions in 1992.